THE ULTIMATE SELLING GUIDE

The
ULTIMATE
SELLING
GUIDE

LLOYD ALLARD

PELICAN PUBLISHING COMPANY
Gretna 2001

This book is dedicated to my brothers, Bill and Ray Allard.
I miss you both and love you.

Library of Congress Cataloging-in-Publication Data

Allard, Lloyd.
    The ultimate selling guide / Lloyd Allard.
       p. cm.
      ISBN 1-56554-423-4 (pbk. : alk. paper)
      1. Selling. I. Title.
    HF5438.25 .A439 2001
    658.85—dc21

                        00-047851

Printed in Canada
Published by Pelican Publishing Company, Inc.
1000 Burmaster Street, Gretna, Louisiana 70053

Contents

Introduction

Thank you for taking some time to read my book, especially if you are a salesperson, sales manager, recruiter, or trainer of sales professionals. I love being a salesman. I love being around other salespeople, talking to them, and writing for them. I think salespeople are the most interesting, fun people in the world, and I don't think they get the recognition or the respect they properly deserve. It is true that "nothing happens until someone sells something."

Do you know why I love being a salesman? It is mainly because I remember what my life was like before I became a salesman. My decision to become a salesman radically altered my life.

I was raised in a one-room tarpaper shack. I can see that dilapidated shack now, sitting precariously on the side of a hill. Can you imagine? There were eleven kids in my family—together with my mom and dad, thirteen people living together in a one-room shack. You talk about poor! We never had decent clothes to wear, and often not enough to eat. We had so many kids sleeping in one bed that if you ever got up in the night, you had to leave a book marker to save your place!

The first job I ever had was cutting wood for a paper mill. It was hot, hard, and dirty work. Did you ever have to cut paper wood for a living? If you haven't, trust me . . . you haven't missed a darn thing.

I have been a salesman, sales manager, recruiter, and trainer since 1959. I've always considered selling to be like a magic carpet for me that allows me to go to exciting places and do wonderful things. I have been a traveling salesman. I have sold from Alaska to Louisiana, the Golden Gate Bridge to the Brooklyn Bridge, and in every town in between. And you know what? I've loved every minute of it!

You've heard of Budweiser, called "The King of Beers"; you've heard of Roy Rogers, known as "The King of Cowboys." Well, my friends call me "The King of Salesmen." If you bought my book and are reading it, then you have just become another friend of mine!

I have written and published three books on sales. The first is titled *Selling*. The second is called *Lessons and Adventures in Sales*. Now, there is this book, *The Ultimate Selling Guide*. All of these books are unlike any others ever written about sales, motivation, or the idea of "Positive Mental Attitude."

The fundamental principles that I first articulated in my previous works are expanded on and developed further in this book. It would be impossible to write an intelligent or profound book on selling without building first upon the foundations I laid in those first two books. They articulate the principles that can make any truly determined person successful in sales. My books also debunk many of the myths that have caused millions of salespeople to fail. At the same time, they are exciting, fun books to read. (In fact, some of you high rollers should think about making a movie based on my books about my life as a salesman!)

Ladies and gentlemen, I can help any salesperson who wants to succeed become more productive and successful. I can also break the expensive cycle of hiring, training, and then losing salespeople that costs most sales companies millions of dollars and causes such a tragic loss in human resources. I *guarantee* success to anyone who will work hard and diligently follow my principles.

Many years ago, I decided to analyze the selling techniques that worked to figure out what made them work. I discovered that there are certain fundamental principles that govern the selling process. When I utilized those principles in my own selling approach, I became very successful. I went from earning around sixty-five thousand dollars a year to an income of several hundred thousand dollars a year.

At the same time, I discovered that much of what we have been teaching salespeople is nothing more than a collection of false and harmful myths. If salespeople actually use half of the techniques they are being taught today, those techniques will inevitably cause them to fail!

Consider for a moment just one common myth that I'll bet everyone reading this book has helped perpetuate at one time or another. Have you ever heard or repeated the old sales training cliche, "If you learn just one good thing from this book, tape, or seminar, that makes it all worthwhile"? Well, I don't want to be unkind, but you know that might just be the dumbest thing anyone has ever said! Think about this with me for a minute. I like Oreo cookies, but I'm not about to jump into a sewer to get one. Why? Because the bad stuff I would take in from the environment of the sewer would do me a lot more harm than the cookie would do me good. Remember that when rat poison is set out as bait, it is *99 percent pure hamburger.*

Now, can you apply that principle to any other decision you make? For example, would you go to a medical school if you knew that half of what they were teaching would kill people?

Of course not! You wouldn't even send your kid to Mr. Goodwrench Auto Mechanics School if half of what they taught caused cars to stop running!

If you can distinguish the difference between the correct and incorrect sales principles, then you probably don't need any training. The tragedy is that millions of salespeople are now working below their capabilities because they are misled by the false, harmful myths they are taught by people who themselves have no idea what truly effective selling principles are.

Millions of people fail in sales every year. They then slink back to their old job at the widget factory, never realizing their potential for success because they were misled by those false and harmful selling myths.

I believe that most salespeople work to about 30 percent of their real ability because of the myths they have been taught. One key reason why there is so much turnover in the recruitment and preparation of new salespeople is *inadequate training*. Listen to me now, sales managers! Much of the inadequacy in your training is not that the training is not there, but that the training you have wastes your new salespeople's time and misdirects their energies by teaching them unsound principles and made-up myth. Most sales companies could save millions of dollars and solve their manpower problems by shifting their emphasis from recruiting to training. Of course, that training should be centered around the principles articulated in my three books.

What follows in this book are just a few of the suggestions, lessons, quotations, observations, and principles I have discovered in sales. This book is a unique, step-by-step guide that can lead anyone to success in sales. How do I know? Because I have recruited, trained, and managed hundreds of successful salespeople. I've seen proof, over and over again, that if you diligently follow the instructions in this book, and if you work hard, you *will* be successful in sales. I guarantee it! Good luck and good selling!

THE ULTIMATE SELLING GUIDE

The Pathway to Success
for a Sales Manager

When I first became a sales manager, I took a good look around me and was appalled at what I saw. I quickly realized that most sales organizations, including our own, were little more than "revolving doors" for salespeople. These companies were hiring salespeople who would stay for a short time, then leave, having suffered yet another professional failure. These salespeople may have contributed a few sales to the organization's bottom line, but they also usually bought supplies with their own money, worked either for low pay or no pay at all, and then they left the job even poorer than they were when they started.

I made a promise to myself. I decided that if I was not able to reverse this trend, I would give up trying to make my living as a sales manager. I was absolutely determined to avoid the trap of building my own career on the shattered careers and lives of other people. I faced formidable barriers in my efforts to reverse the cycle of failure that was plaguing so many salespeople. After careful analysis, I identified four key reasons why so many people were being trapped so easily in this cycle.

1. Many people come into sales totally unprepared for success in the field. They don't know anything about the selling profession, selling techniques, or the tremendous effort that success will require of them in their new job.

2. No one would consider applying for a job as an airline pilot or a chemical engineer without first mastering the necessary skills. For some reason, however, many people believe that professional sales requires no special training, or that it can be learned "on the fly." The sad experiences of many who failed in sales prove again and again that anyone who attempts professional salesmanship with this attitude is almost certainly doomed to fail.

3. In recent years, salespeople have been bombarded with books, seminars, and video or audio tapes offered by sales organizations, all of which try to communicate the same incorrect message . . . that selling is a simple way for anyone to earn obscene amounts of money. They are only interested in selling you books, seminars, tapes, or their products. They are *not* concerned about you being successful in sales.

4. Sales organizations often recruit salespeople by telling them that their product or service is easy to sell. Con men behind the pyramid schemes and other scams flood the marketplace with phony sales opportunities. They work hard to convince us of something that our own simple logic tells us cannot possibly be true . . . namely, that you can earn big rewards by working as little as you want and investing just a small amount your time and energy.

After I analyzed this situation, I decided to try a new approach. I wanted to explore a different path to sales management from any of the directions that had been taken by other managers I'd observed. My new management philosophy was to be based on the following sound selling principles, not made-up hype or theories.

Instead of deluding my new salespeople into thinking that their job would be easy, I decided to convince them that it would take their *very best effort* if they were to succeed. I told them about the long hours of study, practice, and preparation it would take for them to do what looked easy when it was done by experienced and successful salespeople.

Instead of telling these rookies that riches would soon be rolling in, I prepared them for a long period of planning and hard work. I learned long ago that remuneration for any endeavor is based on the "difficulty factor." Put simply, things that are easy to do don't pay very much. On the other hand, career challenges that are difficult and risky, that require preparation and hard work, pay well. To recruit anyone into your sales organization without making sure that he or she fully understands this basic fact of life is a form of professional fraud.

Instead of telling these people that anyone can make it in sales, I advised them that if they wanted to succeed, they would have to study as diligently as any law or premed student. I also made sure they understood that the career they had chosen was so challenging that many of them would fail, despite their efforts. I pointed out the success and failure ratio of those who had come into my sales organization, and made sure they fully understood the implications of those numbers.

Most important of all . . . instead of screening out the candidates whose employment history showed that they were unprepared for success in sales, I focused on three difficult criteria. First, I looked for people who were willing to work hard. Second, I looked for people who were willing to learn. Third, I looked for people who were willing to stick with their new job until they succeeded. I then took those people from wherever they started, whatever their level of success, education, or talent, and I prepared them for real success. I worked as long and hard as necessary to make sure they learned our business and achieved success.

It is extremely challenging to take people "off the street" and teach them how to be successful salespeople. The candidates and I must both understand that there will be many disappointments along the way. Some will do what they think passes for "trying," and they will fail. A few others who have a real work ethic will be willing to invest the energy to succeed at their difficult challenge. As a manager, I had to face the infuriating frustration of putting in many hours, days, and weeks to help a promising new salesperson only to have him or her move on to something else once that person's skills were fully developed.

These are some of the simple, cold-blooded realities of the sales profession. They are not insurmountable barriers, but they are fundamental facts of life that every new sales professional and sales manager must face. When a prospective salesperson realizes what salesmanship really is, both its challenges and opportunities, only then is he or she ready to head into the field with realistic expectations, and a realistic chance of succeeding.

This book is filled with the lessons I've learned in decades of selling and managing salespeople. The suggestions, lessons, quotations, observations, and principles included in this book *will* make you successful in sales and in life if you apply them properly and diligently. I guarantee it. There is no magic here. It is simple logic and applied common sense that I've seen work over and over again. Try it, and see for yourself!

HOW TO GET ANYTHING YOU WANT FOR FREE

May I ask you a personal question? How many of you salespeople are driving around today in a Rolls Royce or a Lamborghini? Really? Why not? To hear some people tell it, we should *all* have the car of our dreams by now! Oh, I bet you're just trying to get one the old-fashioned way. I'll bet you are saving your money to *buy one!*

Hey, wise up! Get smart! Haven't you heard about visualization? Since the 1980s, we have been telling salespeople that if they want a new car, all they have to do is cut out a picture of the car they want, paste it onto their dresser mirror, and visualize having it until, one day, they finally get it.

There are probably half a million salespeople out there today who have a photo clipped from a magazine of a BMW, Porsche, or Corvette pasted onto their mirrors. Every morning these salespeople wake up, glance at the picture, and hope once again that if they only visualize owning their dream car, it will help them actually *get* it.

I heard a guy on the radio in New Orleans, where I was living recently, who has a course on visualization. His pitch went something like this: "You want a new car? More money? A better job? A bigger house? A prettier wife? Just write what you want on a postcard and send it to me along with $39.95 for my training program, and you'll soon be able to get anything you want!"

Well, I sent in for that course. Hey, I am no dummy! I know a good deal when I hear one! I didn't send any money, though. I just *wrote* "$39.95" on the postcard. I told the man that he should *visualize* the hard currency, and send me the course as soon as *he* got the money! You know what? I'm still waiting for that course. . . .

One more thing about those courses you salespeople send away for—you have to listen *very carefully* to learn anything from those danged old "subliminal tapes" that they're selling on radio and TV!

Checkup for a Champion Sales Manager

You can be given no greater honor than to be entrusted with the management of another person's career. Once you've been given that responsibility, you have in your hands not only the welfare of that person, but also that of all those who depend on him or her. All managers should take this responsibility seriously, and prepare themselves to handle it properly.

Remember that the difference between a real leader and a boss is not so much inspiration as it is preparation and perspiration. You should judge yourself by the number and quality of the salespeople you produce, not the number of individuals who are assigned to work for you.

The following is a little checkup test for those of you who already have the critical responsibility of sales management or hope to become a sales manager in the future. Take it now, and see if there is anything you can do to improve your effectiveness.

Read each of the following statements. If you completely agree with the statement, give yourself a 10. If you completely disagree, give yourself a 1. If you are totally neutral about the statement, enter a 5 on the appropriate line. If you somewhat agree or disagree, enter the number you feel is appropriate along the scale of 1 to 10. As you'll see, you are instructed to double your score for five of the questions.

19

The highest possible score you can achieve for this check-up is 300. You can consider yourself as having achieved a "passing" score if your score is 240 or above.

1. I arrive ahead of time, get myself ready, and I'm waiting for people to arrive at work or at sales meetings 100 percent of the time.

(NOTE: Score double for this question.)

Score: _____

2. I evaluate all my salespeople carefully to discover what I can do to help each individual reach his or her full potential.

(NOTE: Score double for this question.)

Score: _____

3. I plan every detail of my sales campaigns.

Score: _____

4. I have all appropriate materials ready and available for my salespeople.

Score: _____

5. I keep accurate business records.

Score: _____

6. I give precise and easy-to-understand directions.

Score: _____

7. I communicate well with my salespeople.

Score: _____

8. I maintain effective control of my salespeople.

Score: _____

9. I have well-defined goals for myself and my salespeople.

Score: _____

10. I delegate authority well without alienating other salespeople.

Score: _____

11. I inspire my salespeople to want to do better.

Score: _____

12. I sometimes invest my personal time and money in my salespeople.

Score: _____

13. I am mentally and physically able to put forth my best effort.

Score: _____

14. I am genuinely concerned about the success of my salespeople—not just for my success but for theirs.
(NOTE: Score double for this question.)
Score: _____

15. I take a personal hand in training my salespeople.
Score: _____

16. I demonstrate leadership by setting high standards of performance for myself.
Score: _____

17. I encourage my salespeople to achieve more and to think more highly of themselves.
Score: _____

18. My salespeople look forward to my sales meetings.
Score: _____

19. I continually educate myself so I can become a better manager.
Score: _____

20. I really know my salespeople. I know them personally, and I am aware of their strengths and weaknesses.
Score: _____

21. I constantly check my salespeople to be sure they are performing properly.
Score: _____

22. I continually educate my salespeople.
Score: _____

23. I am training and grooming selected salespeople to become future managers.
Score: _____

24. I like my salespeople. I enjoy being around them.
(NOTE: Score double for this question.)
Score: _____

25. My salespeople like me and enjoy being around me.
(NOTE: Score double for this question.)
Score: _____

TOTAL SCORE: _____

YOUR SALES MANAGEMENT SKILLS WORKSHEET

In the following box, list the specific management skills you identified from your checkup as areas in need of improvement. Include your personal schedule for achieving your self-development goals. Be specific! (For example, I will achieve "X" by the 15th of next month, or I will achieve "Y" within the next sixty days.)

```
1.

2.

3.

4.

5.

6.

7.

8.

9.

10.

11.

12.

13.

14.
```

How to Be a Salesperson

There is one fundamental truth about salesmanship that must be stated up front: In order to be a great salesperson, you have as much to learn as you would if you wanted to become a great doctor or lawyer. This basic truth frightens so many people that they refuse to believe it. They want to believe that selling can be made easy if you just know the right "tricks" or formulas. So, what do we teach salespeople who don't want to face the real truth? We tell them that you just need to be born with "the gift of gab" or a charismatic personality.

Have you ever heard anyone talk about the idea of a "natural-born salesman"? Think about that for a moment . . . I always thought it would be quite a shock to be the parents of such a creature! Dad goes to the hospital to see his newborn son. Everyone else in his family is either a doctor or lawyer. He looks through the plate-glass window in the maternity ward and is amazed by what he sees. Oh my God! It's a salesman! "Wow," says Dad, "nice briefcase, son! Well, I guess we won't have to be send you off to college. We just give you your sample kit, and off you go, making a lot of money!"

Imagine that you have to go into the hospital for a serious operation. You are probably a little nervous and concerned anyway. Just before they administer the anesthesia, the head of the surgical team standing over you looks down at you on the operating table and says, "Oh, by the way, I should probably tell you that I don't have a degree in medicine. I never went to medical school. I'm just a natural-born doctor."

Well, the truth is that you or anyone else is as likely to be a "natural-born salesman" as you are to be a natural-born brain surgeon. Frankly, I wouldn't want to do business with either one of these people. (You know, when I think back on it now, I figure that's probably why my divorce cost me so much money. I had a natural-born lawyer representing me. I guess I should have gotten one with a law degree!)

Very often, a prospective salesperson will come in to a sales company for an interview. He or she will show great charisma, but it soon becomes evident that he or she relies on this natural attribute for professional success. These are the "natural-born salespeople." When it comes to the hard work, preparation, self-discipline, and persistence that it really takes to succeed, they just don't have it. They are soon off to try something new, exploiting their charisma so they can be a hero for a little while. The promise that they demonstrate in the beginning can never be transformed into sustained success. All too often, it is the natural ability of these people to fascinate others on a superficial level that ends up becoming their greatest liability. Ironically, their natural talents cause them to fail. Why? Because a winning personality can't be solely relied on to produce effective selling. It requires skill . . . and that skill must be *learned*.

HOW MY LIFE WAS CHANGED

In 1978, I underwent a great change in my life. I won't go into all the painful details right now, but it involved a couple of divorces, losing my job, and a few other bad experiences I wouldn't wish on anyone.

I woke up one morning and decided I'd had enough. I was going to start over, and this time, I was going to do things differently. I had grown tired of mediocrity. I wanted to experience genuine success. I wanted to find out once and for all just how good I could be at something. I wanted to take control and do things my way for a change. I decided I didn't care what anyone else thought, whether they liked me or not or approved of what I did. I was determined to blaze my own trail on my own terms.

After reading a book called *How I Raised Myself from Failure to Success in Selling*, by Frank Bettger, I decided to become a direct salesman—a traveling salesman—and a one-call closer.

On the same day I made that all-important career decision, I set two goals for myself. First, I wanted to become the world's *best* direct, traveling salesman. Second, I wanted to be *acknowledged* as the world's best salesman. I've achieved my first objective. I still have a little way to go before I accomplish that second goal.

Since I no longer cared about what anyone else thought, I was able to discard all my inhibitions. This opened up all kinds of opportunities for me that I might never before have considered.

To become the world's best salesman, I tried every sales tactic and technique possible. I wanted to test everything to find out for myself what really worked and what didn't. Sometimes, I made a total fool of myself, but I didn't care. I learned one useful lesson that came in very handy during this time of experimentation: "They won't hit an idiot." Remember that, and don't be afraid to try something new, even if you think it might make you feel foolish or awkward. Until you try something, you never know that it might be just the technique for you!

My technique for transforming myself into the world's greatest salesman can be summarized as follows:

1. I took careful notes and maintained good records of people's reactions to the various sales techniques I tried.

2. I discovered that there are *universal principles* that govern the selling process.

3. I learned that if you stick very closely to the principles that work, you will be successful.

26 THE ULTIMATE SELLING GUIDE

4. I dissected and utilized those successful principles in my sales tactics and techniques.

As I applied the successful principles I uncovered, I found myself experiencing spectacular success. Since that time, I have never had a bad day in direct sales.

As the sales piled up and the money started rolling in, I felt like Alice in Wonderland. I had gone through the looking glass into the wonderful, exciting, and rewarding world of real salesmanship. I still feel that way.

At the same time, I also discovered that much of what was being taught about selling was false and harmful. Most of the made-up myths passing for selling techniques exist only for the purpose of selling gullible salespeople books, tapes, and seminars. I learned quickly the basic truth that when salespeople base their selling tactics on myth, they will fail . . . or, at the very least, they will be less effective than they might otherwise be.

A quick look at selling today will show you that most sales companies are like revolving doors. They hire, train, and then lose masses of people, and make their profits on the short-term successes of eager beginners who have not yet grown tired or bitter. This process is costly to the sales company, and it is devastating to the salespeople who often experience failure after failure.

Selecting a Product
or Service to Sell

This subject is touched on in my first book, *Selling*, but I think a more thorough examination of this topic is appropriate here. The reason I think this issue needs a little more emphasis is the fact that most salespeople give surprisingly little thought to the product or service they will sell beyond asking themselves the question, "Can I make some money selling this product or service?"

The truth is that salespeople should give a *great deal of thought* to this decision. The product or service you sell should complement your personality. Why? It's logical, really. Since we'll spend a lot of our time working with the product or service we sell, it should be something with which we feel comfortable. For example, a friend of mine once sold condoms for a living. He did well financially, but he was always embarrassed to tell people about his career. Some people wouldn't be bothered by that at all, but for this salesman, it was a constant problem. The message here is simple: If the product or service you represent makes you unhappy, you should not sell it. You should also ask yourself whether what you are selling is a short-term fad, or if it will it be around long enough for you to build a professional career out of selling it.

The product or service you sell should also be compatible with your natural abilities. For example, if a selling job you are considering requires physical strength, manual dexterity, or technical skills, be sure to take those factors into consideration when you weigh your decision.

What follows are some principles to consider that are specifically related to selecting the product or service you will sell.

Principles

1. Select only a product or service that you truly believe in. Be sure that you are sincerely convinced that the value of the product or service you are considering actually exceeds the price being asked for it.

2. Never sell any product or service that you don't believe in. If you do, you will spend every day on the job lying . . . not only to your potential customers, but to yourself.

3. Select only products or services that are wanted or needed by enough people to make your efforts profitable.

4. Avoiding being sidetracked by ill-conceived schemes or sales scams. Multilevel network marketing scams abound nowadays, so be wary of any "opportunity" you encounter in which you must first buy a product or service before you can sell it.

5. Products that are "presold" or that are easy to sell almost always offer little remuneration. Conversely, products that are difficult to sell, that take study, practice, and hard work, typically offer much more significant financial rewards.

6. Select a product or service that requires you to study, plan, use your imagination, and work hard in order to sell it. Completely master whatever skills are required to sell the product or service you select, then expect to be paid handsomely for selling it.

7. Greatness is achieved not through an attitude, a single opportunity, good luck, or intelligence. It is achieved through preparation, hard work, and sticking to the task at hand, whatever it may be.

8. Your success does not depend on the number of

opportunities that come your way. It depends instead on whether or not you decide to seize the opportunities that are presented to you, and make the most of them.

BEWARE OF SCAMS

It is heartbreaking for me when I interview salespeople who tell me how their lives have been disrupted and how they've lost money, time, and their dreams because they bought into some sales scam. There are scams in every occupation, of course, but salespeople seem particularly susceptible to being exploited and swindled. Salespeople are typically optimistic, generous, and adventurous, which helps explain why it is easy for them to buy into some scam if they are not careful.

A great scam artist once said, "There is a little larceny in all of us." I believe this is what makes most scams work. Scams are inherently corrupting because people generally buy into one with the idea of scamming others down the road. Of course, no one ever actually says the words, "I am going to scam my friends and relatives," but the intent is clear. The person who becomes involved in a selling scam wants to make big money, and the actual value of the product or service to the end user has little meaning. The important question—indeed, the *only* question—is "Can I make a lot of money doing this?" It is not "Will everyone involved in this business benefit?" Too often, ethical principles are ignored or rationalized away by people when they are blinded by greed. It is easy to convince yourself that everything is okay when big dollar signs are dancing in front of your eyes.

Principles

1. A plague has descended on the profession of salesmanship. It may go by many different names, but it is always the same thing . . . multilevel network marketing.

2. In my opinion, multilevel network marketing by any name and in all its various forms, is in and of itself, a scam.

3. Multilevel network marketing scams are all basically the same. A few people at the top suck the money, energy, and enthusiasm out of thousands of people at the bottom.

4. Does the company you are considering offer products or services that you must first buy and then sell yourself to people who will, in turn, have to sell those same products or services yet again? If so, you are probably dealing with a scam.

5. Does the company promise great rewards for an investment of very little money, time, work, and effort? If so, you are probably dealing with a scam.

6. Can almost anyone do the job? Can it be done without preparing or learning, and still hold out the promise of a high income? If so, you are probably dealing with a scam.

7. Generally, the biggest inducement that a scam uses to suck you into its web is the offer of a thinly disguised opportunity to scam other people out of their money. This strategy seldom works to your benefit, however. The con men at the top will get your money, and will usually also find a way to get the money you manage to swindle out of your friends and relatives.

8. Con men often look important, dress well, and appear self-confident . . . but they are still con men. Avoid them. Never make money at someone else's expense.

9. "I know he's a wolf," said Riding Hood, "but Grandma, dear, he smells so good." (Burma Shave)

10. Much of what is taught to salespeople today is hype and myth. It is designed to sell books, tapes, and seminars only . . . nothing else. Most of this material will actually make you fail rather than succeed.

11. Are any of these points upsetting you? If they are, maybe it's because I am shedding light on some of your activities. The hit dog always yelps.

12. When you have lost all the money, time, and faith you have invested in a selling scam, and you will lose them all, look around you. Look into the faces of your family,

your friends, and the acquaintances whom you've involved in your scheme, and think about all the unhappiness you have caused.

13. God gives us our whole life one present at a time.

14. When you are involved in any multilevel marketing scheme, you experience only two happy days. The first is the day you get in. The second is the day you finally get out, and finally get rid of all the stuff!

15. Before you invest in any plan you think might be a selling scam, be sure to talk with someone who was once involved in it but is now completely out.

16. Whenever you receive a letter that says something like, "You've already won a lot of money!" or "You're our grand prize winner!", just pitch it into the trash.

17. You can never judge a scam by the people who endorse it. Unscrupulous scam operators pay big money to celebrities for endorsements, and those celebrities often don't know or understand that they are being used as "fronts" for a fraud.

18. Fools do not respond to simple logic. (That is why they are fools!)

19. "A fool and his money are soon parted." Unfortunately, he has generally parted with his money before he meets you!

20. "The exact opposite of what is generally believed is often the truth." Jean De La Bruyere (1645-96)

21. The first question you should ask yourself when presented with an opportunity that sounds too good to be true is this: "If this deal is so good, why would they let me in on it?"

Standing by the Stuff

In the years I've been in sales, I've seen many salespeople come and go. In fact, I've even seen entire sales organizations come and go! Looking back, I'm surprised to see which ones become vastly successful and which did not. I believe I have discovered one single characteristic that is common to all *truly* successful people in any career, but especially to salespeople.

When I started in sales, I wanted to become a superstar. I wanted to break records, win contests, and earn the admiration of my peers and managers. Above all, I wanted to make *big money*. After I'd been working in sales for a short while, I was introduced to a salesman who seemed to have everything I was looking for. He dressed like a millionaire, drove a big, expensive car, and constantly beamed charisma and excitement. His name was Chris. When I first met him, he held almost all the sales records in our company. After we were introduced to one another, he grabbed my hand and said, "God is great, our company is great, and I'm great, too! How are you?"

I felt terrific just being around this guy. Chris told me that he was the greatest salesman our company ever had and he was going to become the greatest manager our company had ever seen. It soon became apparent, however, that Chris was a superstar with no staying power. He would achieve things, but then he would indulge in long periods of inactivity. He couldn't stick with his job long enough to become a real success. Well, Chris isn't with our company anymore. He ended up working for me, and frankly, he proved to be more of a pain than an asset.

Most of the "superstar" salespeople I've ever known didn't go on to become very successful in sales, management, or life. They generally lacked one characteristic that truly successful salespeople share. On the other hand, some of today's top managers were not even taken seriously as salespeople when they were out in the field just a few years ago. Some had a difficult time being hired, and then even more difficulty just holding on to their jobs. And yet, these people are now earning extremely high incomes. They and their families are set for life. What is it that these people have that others do not? What is that one trait that all champions have in common? Is there a single, definable characteristic that distinguishes the real winners in every field from all the rest?

In my years of hiring and training salespeople, I've met many who come to the job with lots of native talent. Some also come with considerable experience. Some are financially well off, while others start off flat broke. Our company has some salespeople on staff who have Ph.D. degrees, while others have practically no education. As you might expect, these people have a wide range of personality types. Some are very outgoing while others seem extremely introverted. Viewed in a certain way, these people seem to have almost nothing in common.

A person's outward character traits, professional skills, and individual circumstances can certainly have an important impact on his ability to do his job well. However, there is one more attribute that far exceeds any other in importance. That attribute is *tenacity* . . . the ability and willingness to stick with something until the challenge is overcome and the ultimate victory is achieved. If you possess this trait, you can succeed at anything.

Think about this in terms of our country's recent history.

All would agree that the United States controls the most powerful military force on Earth. If firepower and technology were the only factors needed to win wars, this nation would be invincible. Still, we lost the Vietnam War. Why? Because the Vietnamese people were willing to fight longer and endure more pain than we were.

In the Old Testament, King David tells us in 1 Sam. 30:24 that those who stand by their stuff should get the same reward as those who conquer. The person who has the ability to stick with something until he or she conquers it is able to succeed at anything. Whether you call it determination, stick-to-it-ive-ness, or tenacity, it is *the* key element in becoming a success at anything.

All too often these days, people spend their free time seeking out easy solutions to problems. People want to "get rich quick." This attitude has provided a fertile breeding ground for "pyramid schemes" and other corrupt practices that feed off human greed by promising great rewards for little effort.

The truth, of course, is something we should have all learned early in our lives. *Nothing truly worth having in life comes quickly or easily.* Once you accept this simple truth, you're ready to follow this surefire recipe for success in sales.

First, think for a moment. You will spend approximately one-third of the time left in your life working at your career. Of all the decisions you will have to make in your life, your career choice is probably among the two or three most important. That being the case, ask yourself . . . exactly where will you be five years from now or ten years from now?

As a recruiter and trainer of salespeople, I can tell you without hesitation that the single characteristic I look for above all others is the sales candidate's ability to stick with whatever he does until he gets the job done. Consider the following:

1. If I know a person will stick with me, then I also know that I can afford to invest my time in him.

2. If I am sure that the person is going to stay with me, then I can confidently invest my money in his training.

3. If this person sticks around for a long time, then I'm likely to want and expect him to become a manager in my organization.

As I noted earlier, too many salespeople today are looking for an easy way to sell and a quick way to make money. Sales programs that are quick and easy, or programs that can be implemented by anybody, are for peddlers, snowbirds, and job hoppers! Those jobs are usually nothing more than scams that earn little or no money for anyone other than the person who sets up the scam in the first place. You will almost certainly never build a future in such a job. Instead, find something else that will demand your best efforts. Then, stick with it until you completely master it.

Here are some basic steps you should take if you want to be successful in your sales career.

1. *Study salesmanship.* Learn the principles of sales that are described in my other two books and this book. Learn to be a great salesperson (which, of course, also means learn how to be a great actor). Then, stick with it diligently until you have mastered your trade.

2. *Learn the fine art of closing a sale.* In truth, no one ever *completely* masters this skill. Closing is a process that you should study throughout your professional lifetime if you are to master it as much as possible. You see, closing is not only an art . . . it is also a science. A salesperson must apply many different skills before he or she can implement and master the proper closing process. Never forget, however, that closing is also payday for salespeople. That fact alone is reason enough for every salesperson to work hard on it and stick with it until he or she has it mastered.

3. *Know your company, and know everything you can learn about its products or services.* Don't ever settle for knowing

just enough to "get by." Learn until you become the acknowledged expert on your company, its products, and its services.

4. *Study management.* Learn how to recruit, motivate, and manage people. Practice public speaking and all the other skills necessary to manage a sales organization. Look at each salesperson as an opportunity for you to bring out his best.

5. *Always be honest.* Be honest with your customers, fellow workers, and company. Most important of all, be honest with yourself. Be honest even when no one will ever know about it but you. That kind of honesty builds character.

6. *Work harder and longer than anyone else in your organization.* Work until you are number one. Obtaining your goals is very much like buying something at an auction. The only one who gets the prize is the one who is willing to pay the most.

Within the next five years, some of you will be earning forty to fifty thousand dollars a month. Others among you will have failed. *All* of us have the ability and the opportunity to reap the benefits of this fantastic profession if we simply apply these six principles. You *can* have it all. You can be part of a big organization, be a top professional salesperson, and be secure for the rest of your life! Why not start toward that goal today?

Selecting a Company to Represent

In my book *Selling*, I also touched on the importance to salespeople of selecting the right company, but as I've watched phony selling "opportunities" popping up like mushrooms everywhere these days, I thought that a more thorough treatment would be appropriate here.

A big mistake many salespeople make is not exercising adequate care when they select the company they want to represent. This decision is almost as important for salespeople as the decision of their marriage partner. And, as many have learned over the years, instant gratification of your needs is not a good foundation for a long-lasting relationship in marriage or sales.

As I've said before, you must put a lot of time and effort into your career if you are going to have great success. You must make sure the time and effort you invest will pay you the long-term benefits you desire. Your welfare and the welfare of all those who rely on you will depend on your success in making the right choice.

Principles

1. When selecting the company you want to represent, be sure to choose an organization you can trust and in which you can take pride.

2. Make sure the company is stable. Assure yourself that

the firm will be there when it's time for you to reap the rewards for your efforts.

3. In most selling situations, you can earn a lot more money working on commission than you would if you drew a regular salary.

4. There is no true security in drawing a salary. With the possible exceptions of pope and Supreme Court justice, no job is guaranteed to anyone for a lifetime. The only security you really have is your ability to do your job well.

5. Small salaries, insurance, etc., are sometimes referred to as "Golden Handcuffs." They will keep you in a low-paying job and rob you of your chance to really succeed if you are not careful.

6. Don't trade the unlimited opportunity afforded to you by working on a commission for the false security and financial limitations of working on a salary.

7. Do what you can to have your remuneration agreement put in writing so that you cannot be cheated out of the fruits of your labors.

8. Once you've found a company in which you can take pride, be loyal to it, and remain dependably loyal for as long as you are associated with the organization.

9. Never run down your company, co-workers, territory, or remuneration. All too often, such complaints are made by salespeople who are seeking excuses for their failure. Also, if you display a negative attitude toward your job, it will inevitably turn your family against your company. When they, in turn, reinforce your attitude, they will unwittingly sap your motivation and energy. This will make it far more difficult for you to succeed.

10. Remember that "familiarity breeds contempt." Also, recognize the wisdom of the old saying, "The grass is always greener on the other side of the fence." Don't allow yourself to become so familiar with your job that you take it for granted, become contemptuous about it, and forget how important it really is.

11. When we take pride in our company, we invariably project that pride to our customers.

12. Keep a close and careful eye on your corporate expenditures. Too many salespeople become careless about such things as telephone charges, car expenses, room-service bills, and other costs that are passed on to their company. If you become careless in this area, your company may decide that it isn't safe to trust you with bigger and more important responsibilities. True professionalism and good character demand that we be more conscientious with other people's money than we are with our own.

13. Cooperate with your superiors. Offer your boss the same kind of support that you hope to receive when you become the boss. Remember . . . you won't suddenly become a "team player" just because you're made captain of the team!

14. Every opportunity we receive is accompanied by a corresponding responsibility.

15. "Ask not what your company can do for you, but what you can do for your company." (With apologies to JFK)

16. Never let yourself forget how you felt when you didn't have a job.

17. Those who complain the most about being unemployed always tend to be the ones who did the least to keep their jobs.

18. If you should ever reach the point where you can no longer represent your company with pride and respect, don't complain. Just quit.

STARTING A CAREER IN SALES

When you begin a new career, it is important to start off on the right foot. The decisions you make in these early days will have a longer-lasting impact on your overall success than those you make later in your career. The direction you take and the friendships you make in the beginning are very important to your overall success. You must be willing to work long hours and burn a lot of energy to get your new career off to a good start. The impression you make on your co-workers in the first stage of your career will determine how you will be treated for a long time to come.

Principles

1. Listen to your sales manager. Solicit his or her advice, and do whatever he or she tells you to do within reason. Of course, you should never let anyone in a position of power take advantage of you or make you do anything that you know is not right. Bear in mind that sales managers are evaluated, and often paid, based on how well their field representatives perform. It is therefore in your manager's best interest to help you succeed!

2. Observe the other salespeople in your organization carefully. Keep your eyes open at all times. Study how your co-workers do their jobs. Pay particular attention to the "star performers" in your office.

3. If you are a seasoned sales veteran, resist the temptation to talk about your past accomplishments. Let the senior salespeople in your organization be the heroes now. When you let them shine, they will be much more likely to teach you the "tricks of the trade" that have worked for them. If you bide your time and keep an eye on the star performers in your office, you can be confident that your time to bask in the sun will surely come.

4. You will learn more about yourself from a person who has bad manners than you ever will from a sophisticated, well-bred person with good manners.

5. You will learn more by listening to complaints than you will by listening to compliments.

6. Remember, most of the compliments you get while training are meant to encourage you. Don't let them go to your head.

7. Always look for positive characteristics in everybody

and everything. Ignore any negatives you may hear about anybody or anything until you have completely mastered your craft. Then, and only then, will you be in a position to make intelligent judgments about your new situation and the people you find there.

8. Keep in mind that the experienced and successful salespeople in your organization have already learned their skills. For that reason, you have to work harder and put in longer hours than they do if you are to succeed in the same organization. If you only put in the same amount of effort that others in your office do, you may be able to keep up. However, you will have to consistently work harder and put in more time than any of them if you hope to surpass them! Buy your own success by investing your time and effort. The payoff will be well worth it.

9. Volunteer to do extra duty. You may not realize it, but when you start out in a new organization, your lack of experience creates extra work for others in your office. Some people have to take time away from their own assignments to train you, oversee you, and correct your mistakes. Do what you can to compensate them for this investment by doing more than your share whenever you can.

10. Don't be gullible. Unfortunately, experienced salespeople sometimes take advantage of new employees who are eager to please their boss and co-workers. Try to avoid lending money, paying for drinks or meals, or taking on any other unwarranted expenses that can drain your resources as you start your new career. Learn to say no, firmly and clearly.

11. For the professional salesperson, success is easy to define. When you make a sale, you've succeeded. When you don't make a sale, you've failed. It's that simple! Work on your presentation constantly, making it better and better. Then, keep on making it to your customers as often as you must to be successful!

12. When you work hard, make a meaningful investment

of time, prepare carefully, study hard, and pursue your goals tenaciously, you'll quickly find that no other career rewards you as handsomely as does sales.

13. Sometimes, an individual is promoted solely on the basis of his or her talent. For every one of those, however, there are thousands of others who are promoted because they've worked a little harder than their peers. Sometimes, a person fails because he or she doesn't have enough talent. But for every one of those, there are thousands of others who fail because they didn't prepare themselves properly and didn't work hard enough at their jobs.

14. Develop a sense of urgency, enthusiasm, and intensity about everything you do. Don't wait for things to happen to you. Study, prepare, and work as though there were no tomorrow.

15. Select winners to imitate. Avoid any negative salespeople you may meet, and avoid taking any advice from salespeople who are not doing well.

16. You will always be a winner if you do your best.

17. Accept constructive criticism gratefully. Always use such criticism to improve yourself whether it is given sincerely (as it usually is) or otherwise. Remember that it is difficult to offer helpful suggestions to people, especially if the advice is about personal matters such as appropriate dress or grooming habits. Keep that in mind when you are on the receiving end of such criticism. If you do not respond well to the advice you receive, you will eventually cut off your so]urces of a very valuable commodity!

18. Any new salesperson who wants to succeed should put on blinders that shut out all distractions. Don't let yourself be sidetracked! Master your presentation until you can deliver it perfectly. Master your delivery, and say it convincingly. Work toward mastering every aspect of your business from the very start.

19. Having the desire to learn is more important than having an education.

20. Knowing how to find the answers is more important than knowing the answers.

21. Always give your company a full day's work for the full day's pay you will receive . . . especially if you are paid on a commission basis!

22. Never deal with your company dishonestly in any way.

23. Never waste your company's resources. Brochures, supplies, and other goods should be preserved whenever possible. You can freely waste your own resources if you are inclined to do so, but jealously guard against wasting what others have entrusted to your care.

24. Your company creates the income that supports you and your family. Think for a moment . . . where would you be without it?

25. Your company has invested a great deal of time and money in you. That company has every right to expect you to be a profit-making part of the corporate team.

26. When you joined your company, you agreed to specific terms with your employer. So long as you continue to accept the money that your employer offers you, you should always honor those terms fully.

27. Consider the things that are good or unique about the conditions under which you work. Then, consider the things that are good or unique about the people with whom you associate only because of your job.

28. So long as your company is fair to you, you should be fair to it. If you ever conclude that it is no longer possible for you to be fair, then quit your job and move on to something different.

29. Under no circumstances should you allow an unfair situation to make a crook out of you.

30. Your company probably has certain unique perks and opportunities that it offers to you and your fellow workers. Don't ever take these for granted. Appreciate them, and think about what they really mean to you.

31. Whenever you find yourself thinking that your job

is tough or unpleasant, remind yourself of this basic fact: You could be hauling heavy sacks of cotton or shoveling horse manure instead of selling. Things could always be worse than they are. Value what you have!

32. Your company could be as critical, unforgiving, and inconsiderate of you as you sometimes are of it . . . but it probably isn't.

33. If you ever find yourself having difficulty appreciating your company, try doing these simple mental exercises. Remember how you felt when you were stuck in a boring, dead-end, low-paying job. Remember how you felt when you wanted the position you now have, but you weren't able to attain it. Consider what you'd have to do and how hard you'd have to work to achieve that position you desire.

34. If your company is honest and reliable, if it provides you with a good work plan, then treat it with the respect it deserves. Honor it and be loyal to it. Don't ever tear it down. Both you and your company will reap the rewards of mutual respect!

35. The number-one reason salespeople fail is because they don't work hard enough and long enough to succeed. More than everything else I have said to you, listen to this: Work harder than you ever thought it was possible for you to work. Work harder than anyone else is willing to work, and work longer hours than anyone else is willing to work, and soon others will be working for you.

36. If the top salesperson in your organization is 30 percent better than you, and you make 50 percent more calls than that top person makes, you will outsell him or her 20 percent.

SOME SPECIAL THOUGHTS FOR SALES MANAGERS

37. True leadership consists of convincing others to have confidence in you by first convincing them to have

confidence in themselves. Do you consider each salesperson on your team as a personal responsibility by asking yourself, "How can I change that person for the better?" and "How far can I help that salesperson go?"

38. Instead of deluding your new salespeople into believing that their job will be easy, convince them from the beginning that it will take a lot of time and their very best effort if they are to succeed. Instead of telling them that riches will soon be rolling in, prepare them for a long period of planning and hard work.

39. Instead of telling these people that anyone can make it in sales, advise them of the hard fact that they'll have to study as hard as any law or premed student if they want to succeed. Make sure they understand that a sales career is so challenging that many of them will fail despite their best efforts.

40. A plastic dog will never attract fleas or shed hair on the couch. It will also never warn you of danger, or greet you at the door with a wagging tail.

41. Always be more interested in helping, improving, and managing the careers of your salespeople than you are in earning money from their labors.

42. Most important of all, instead of screening out the people whose history might indicate that they are unprepared or unsuccessful, focus on two different criteria. First, look for people who are willing to work hard. Second, look for people who are willing to learn. When you find them, take these people at any level of success, education, or talent and prepare them for real success.

43. When you are older and look back on your career, you will feel more pride and satisfaction when you remember the people you have helped become successful than you will when you think about your own success.

44. Hiring a well-trained, organized, motivated salesperson is never as personally gratifying as helping a less successful person become successful.

45. Despite what you may have heard, prostitution is not the world's oldest profession. As the saying goes, "nothing happens until someone sells something." If that is true, then that makes salesmanship—or saleswomanship—the world's oldest profession. Think about it!

46. Don't ever settle for mediocrity just because your peers may be mediocre performers. Remember that "in the land of the blind, the one-eyed man is king!" (Erasmus)

47. Before you can do great things, you must first learn to do small things in a great way. You will probably never get the opportunity to do anything great if you aren't doing well what you're supposed to be doing right now.

48. None of us is ever as smart as all of us! Listen to everyone. You can never know who might have the next great idea.

49. Treat others in such a way that they will like themselves better when they are around you.

50. "Who dares nothing need hope for nothing." (Don Carlos)

The Sale: How Do You Cut the Pie?

To be successful, every salesperson must understand the key elements that make up a sale, as well as their relative importance. There are various ways to build value, create urgency, etc., that are unique to every product and service. However, the overriding principles of effective sales are universal, regardless of the product or service being sold. What follow are a few thoughts on the "fundamental components" that can be found in every sale.

VALUE

The only reason anyone ever buys anything is for the *value* he perceives in owning it. As salespeople, therefore, we must master the art of building value. The essence of effective salesmanship is to find out what is of value to your customer and incorporate that value into the product or service you are offering.

There are many ways to say the same thing to a customer in order to build value. For example, suppose you are talking to a businessperson who has made it clear that he or she is looking for something that will help him or her make or save money. You might build value for that prospective customer by making any of the following points:

THE SALE
HOW DO YOU CUT THE PIE?

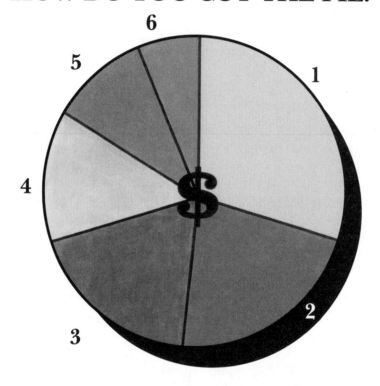

NOTE - PLACE THE VARIOUS ELEMENTS THAT MAKE UP A SALE
IN THEIR PROPER ORDER IN THE PIE. GIVE THE MOST
IMPORTANT ELEMENTS THE BIGGEST PIECE OF PIE.

PRICE - TRUST - VALUE
CONSTRUCTION - CLARITY - URGENCY

THE SALE
HOW DO YOU CUT THE PIE?

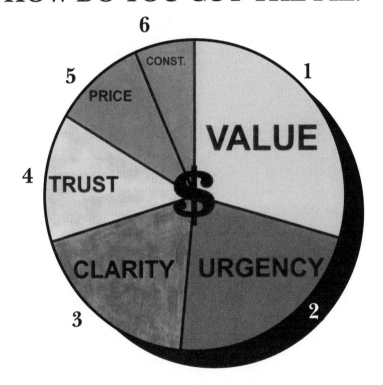

THE PROPER ORDER IS:

#1 VALUE #2 URGENCY #3 CLARITY
#4 TRUST #5 PRICE #6 CONSTRUCTION

1. "This product or service will make or save you a lot of money."

2. "This product or service will make or save you enough money to pay your rent."

3. "Think how much money you would be able to save if you didn't have to pay any rent for the next twenty years! That is what this product or service will do for you; it will *more* than pay your rent!"

4. Appealing to the customer's ego is another value-building technique we should master. If you can get your customers to see their friends, family, peers, and competitors taking note of their success, you can sell them almost anything.

5. The fear of losing business, falling behind the competition, not keeping up with the Joneses, etc., is sometimes a stronger reason for the customer to buy than the prospect of making more money or having more success.

6. Identify your customers' dreams. Rekindle those dreams and incorporate them in the presentation of your product or service. Salespeople who learn this tactic can sell almost anyone almost anything, at almost any price.

7. When the value of your product or service exceeds the price in the mind of your customer, the customer buys. If the customer does not buy, you did not cause the value of your product or service to exceed its price in his or her mind.

If I have done anything well as a salesman, it is causing my customers to see, feel, and experience the benefits they will gain by owning my product. I also tap into their egos by having them see their friends, peers, family, and competition marveling at their success. Building value is our stock in trade, and we should master the art.

URGENCY

It is essential in most sales situations, and desirable in all sales situations, to create urgency. The most important factor in creating urgency in selling is your ability to persuade your customer that his or her most logical next step is to *buy now*. To be truly effective in sales, you must master the art of creating urgency. If you take this one step further and decide that you want to be a "one-call closer," you must make a promise to yourself that you will never make a callback to any customer for any reason.

Many different sales "closes" intended to create urgency can be tailored for every product or service. You should carefully and creatively think of the various ways you have available to you to create urgency in your unique situation. The following are some examples of ways to create urgency that you can use to spark your own ideas about this important selling technique.

1. One effective way to create urgency is to give your customer a discount for helping you develop new leads. This tactic is particularly effective because from your customer's point of view, it is both logical and believable.

2. Offer to give your customer a sample product or an extended service plan if he or she will buy today. Giving your customer a free product or service is a way for you to lower your price without lowering the value.

3. Your customers will never believe that you are giving them a special deal if they cannot see what you are getting out of it. Your customers must see you build value for yourself as well as for them as you lower your price. For example, you might say something like, "Mr. Customer, the reason I'm giving you this special deal today is because you are going to help me get a lot of leads." Your offer then makes sense to the customer, and that groundwork of trust makes a "yes" decision much easier for him or her to make.

CLARITY

Whenever customers are confused or unsure during a

presentation, they will generally not buy. If you don't make the terms of the sale clear, you will have many cancellations and many unhappy customers. The longer I'm in sales, the more I realize the value of clarity in sales presentations. I have found that when I work with my salespeople on making the conditions of the sale clear, their sales always go up.

1. You are a professional. Your job is not just to tell the customer the whole truth about your product or service, but to go even farther by making sure that he understands all the truth. The customer must know and understand all the terms of the sale, the delivery time, and the total cost before the final agreement is reached.

2. When we fail to spell out the conditions of a sale, when we blur the details, we lose business. As a rule, our customers are as smart as we are. They can usually spot a phony and a con man. And if the customer cannot spot a crook, your boss generally can! Your career in sales will be short if you don't tell your customers the truth.

TRUST

The nature of the selling business requires a high degree of trust between the customer and the salesperson. Your customers must trust you and the company you represent.

1. The best way to evoke trust is to be absolutely trustworthy.

2. You should expect to be trusted. Showing your customers some form of identification, calling your company to verify your identity, or doing anything like this to prove you are honest generally does not help. Why? Because when you demonstrate uncertainty about your own trustworthiness by offering external proofs, your customer will only become more suspicious of you, not more assured.

3. Knowing your business and being consistently professional evokes trust. Everyone wants to do business with a professional who is confident about what he is doing.

4. Doing only what is best for your customer and for your company always evokes trust. It also helps communicate to your customer how important the sale is to you.

PRICE

When a customer believes that the value of your product exceeds the price you are asking for it, that customer will buy. Remember that there is a definite limit to how far you can lower your price, but there is *no* limit to how much you can build value. If there is one foolproof way to evaluate the effectiveness of a professional salesperson, it is by how well he or she builds value. In fact, building value is the key to all selling. There are as many different ways to build value as there are customers. You should make developing the skill of building value effectively a lifetime pursuit, and master the art of lowering your price only sparingly and slowly (making your customer understand the importance of a lower price).

1. Every time you lower your price, you lower the value of your product or service in the mind of your customer. You must compensate for this fact by building more value in your customer's mind.

2. The price of your product or service is whatever you decide it is. If you are convinced it is worth more than you are asking for it, you will be very convincing.

3. Since closing the sale is payday for most salespeople, you should master the art of pricing your product. Since giving a discount is a big part of selling many products and services, you should practice this part of your presentation until you can make the figures jump through hoops.

CONSTRUCTION

All good salespeople tell their customers everything they need to know about construction—the unique features of their product or service—so the customers can make an intelligent buying decision. Every good salesperson also knows when to shut up and move on to more important things . . . like what the customers will get out of the product or service once they make the buying decision!

1. Those who think they are salespeople but who talk too much about construction are order takers, not salespeople. Order takers are boring and don't ever make much money. The ratio of talking about value (or benefits to the buyer) to construction (or features) should be about ten to one in favor of value.

2. As the old saying goes, "construction does not lead to seduction." Never expect a customer to be won over by your description of features alone.

3. The weakest approach to selling any product or service is construction. Unfortunately, it is the point where many salespeople or order takers spend most of their time.

There are many other elements to making an effective sale. These include excitement, appearance, effective prospecting, acting, reliability, and so on. As professional salespeople who want to succeed, we should all master every aspect of our business.

Tools of the Trade

When I was a kid, I enjoyed watching a television Western now considered a classic of television's golden age. The show was called Have Gun Will Travel. The hero of this series, Paladin, wasn't much in the way of either looks or smarts. He never dazzled you with his eloquent speech. In fact, he didn't speak very much at all. The plot lines of this show weren't intellectually challenging mysteries. Still, you could always be sure of one thing. When Paladin went for that "big iron" on his hip, you always knew that somebody was in big trouble. Paladin could use that "hog leg," the tool of his trade, better than anyone. I still remember it clearly. The big gun jumped out of his holster like a bolt of lightning, and then *wham!* You were dying even before you knew you'd been hit.

Selling, as you should already know, is a difficult trade. When I teach sales, I spend a lot of time talking about the importance of mastering the presentation and all of the other elements necessary to becoming a real sales professional. Right now, I'd like to take a closer look at the tools that a salesperson has at his or her disposal . . . tools that, like Paladin's gun, are essential to getting the job done, effectively and professionally.

In this lesson, we'll consider one of the most neglected aspects of our business, that is, the physical, tangible tools that salespeople use to help them with their sales presentation. Mastering the use of these tools is as important to you and your sales efforts as it is for a soldier to master his rifle or for a mechanic to master a wrench. Surprisingly, this point is often overlooked by salespeople. That can be a big mistake . . . one I don't ever want you to make! Pay close attention to what follows. You may be surprised how your sales volume will rise when you "get back to the basics" and use the tools of our trade properly! Of course, many tools are unique to particular selling situations. You must use your imagination to decide what tools you can incorporate into your own sales. The following are a few ideas that I've incorporated into my selling situations to make myself more effective.

YOUR SAMPLE

If your company has given you a sample to use in your sales presentation, consider yourself very fortunate! Used properly, a sample can improve your chances of making a sale by 25 to 30 percent. Given this fact, it is obvious that proper use of a sample should be both understood and mastered. Sales managers, if it's possible for you to provide a sample to your salespeople that will demonstrate your product or service, you should do so. The results will be well worth the expense!

I've been able to hold the attention of a barroom full of drunks using my sample. I love my sample and treat it as though it were made of gold. After all, it's helped me earn plenty of "gold" over the years. I keep it clean and in good working order. I truly believe that if I ever had a selling job that didn't provide me with a sample, I would think up some way to make or simulate one. My experience has shown me that the perfected use of a sample can provide courage and effectiveness to even the most ordinary or uninspired salespeople. *You should absolutely master the use of your sample!*

1. Your customer will usually take your sample as seriously

as you do. Remember that your customer has never seen you or your sample before. If you act as though you are overly familiar with the sample and take it for granted, your customer will sense your attitude and will not be impressed by what he is seeing and hearing. Excitement and intensity are a must in your demonstration. Halfway measures never work!

2. Your sample must be used effectively.

3. Your sample must be used often.

4. Your sample must be used consistently.

5. When done properly, you can use your sample to totally control not only your customer but any large crowd of people that may also be in the room when you make your presentation.

6. Don't hit your sample to show how durable it is. That only makes you look like a peddler.

7. Don't sit your sample on the floor unless it is a floor model. If you do, you depreciate its value.

8. Expect everyone to take your sample seriously by treating it as if it is important.

9. Master every description and gesture that has to do with the demonstration and explanation of your sample just as if you were an actor putting on a play.

YOUR PROPOSAL

1. Think of your proposal as a tangible product or service. Hold it over your head. Show it around to everyone in the room. Cause the customer to "see" your product or service as he looks at your proposal. Just like your sample and brochure book, treat your proposal with respect. Why? Because in the final analysis, your proposal has whatever value you think it has. Let your actions communicate the significance of your proposal to your customers.

2. You should never let yourself become bogged down in your presentation, but you should never rush ahead,

either. The more time you are able to take, the more important your proposal will seem to the customer. But be careful . . . presenting a proposal is a lot like baking a cake. If you bake it for too long, it will be ruined. But if you bake it for too little time, it will also be ruined.

3. Present your proposal with great confidence and pride in what you have to offer. Don't be shy or humble at this point. Expect compliance. Expecting your customer to answer "yes" is the best way to get "yes" for your answer.

4. Don't try to accommodate your customers by reacting positively to whatever whims they may express. Give your customers what they need, but not everything they say they want. Remember that customers often don't know what is best for them. That's why they need you, the professional salesperson! Your customer wants to know that you know what is best, and even if he may never say it, he also wants to know that you have enough integrity to insist on doing things right.

5. Practice and perfect presenting your proposal for the maximum dramatic effect. This will help communicate the value you place on your proposal and clarify your own attitude toward its value. This will, in turn, communicate that value into the mind of your customer and establish itself there as the "right" attitude toward your offer.

YOUR BROCHURE BOOK

A sales prop can take many different forms. It could be your brochure book, photographs, or a simple list of figures on a piece of paper. It might be a sketched chart. It could be a prop that gets and holds the attention of the customer. The options for the form a sales prop can take are almost limitless. As a rule, most salespeople don't use enough imagination and creativity when they put together their proposal. In fact, the use of a good prop can make a sales proposal a work of art. Whether your customer ultimately buys or not, you should always give him a show worth watching.

There is a proper, professional way to hold a brochure book. If you are right handed, grip the left side of the book in your left hand as you face your customer. Place the right side against your chest. This leaves your right hand free to point, make gestures, and turn the pages. Holding the brochure book properly must be practiced to be mastered, just like holding a golf club.

Your brochure-book presentation can be the "make or break" point in any sale. That's because this is the point where you are most likely to lose the customer's attention. As you show your brochure book, keep in mind the old vaudeville axiom, "leave the audience wanting more." You should walk the customer through your book with intensity and evident pride. Note the following points:

1. Never let the customer thumb through your brochure book. Keep complete control of it throughout your presentation. Remember that the way you treat this book conveys your sense of its value, and the value you place on its contents, to the customer. If you treat it casually, the customer will believe that it and the information it contains are of little value. Treat it with great respect and protect it closely. The customer will then share your respect for your product.

2. When discussing a specific page in the book, don't have your fingers poised to turn to the next page. This can cause your customer to lose interest in what you're saying as he or she starts wondering what's on the next page.

3. Don't ever bore your customers by overexplaining every point and page. If you notice that your customers look at their watches while you speak, you are boring them. If they check their watches to see if they are still running, you can be certain that you're boring them to death!

4. Keep all of your points clear and brief. Don't mumble or overelaborate.

5. Don't ask the customer for his or her opinion about anything. A salesperson who seeks the opinions or approval

of customers conveys uncertainty. This, of course, works against the salesperson.

6. Keep your presentation moving forward at all times. Don't allow yourself to get "bogged down" or sidetracked. Stay with your script, and say what you have to say with authority.

PHOTOGRAPHS

Remember what your mother used to tell you? "A picture is worth a thousand words." People prefer to buy something they have *seen* . . . so if you can't show them the thing itself, show them pictures of what you are selling!

It is very difficult, or even impossible, for some customers to visualize what a thing looks like without seeing a sample, drawing, or photograph of it. Salespeople who think they can create "word pictures" for the customer that lets him see in his mind's eye what they are describing verbally are usually wrong. Let's face it . . . most salespeople aren't poets, and most customers aren't all that good at imagining things! Samples or illustrations help make this part of the selling process easier for everybody.

1. Another version of the old cliche that is just as true is one good picture is worth a thousand poor ones! And one large photograph is more effective than many smaller ones. Make sure the pictures you show are the best and biggest they can be.

2. Be sure to let everyone in the room see your pictures. Then, solicit their approval to reinforce the points you are making with your prospect.

3. Photographs that aren't directly related to your product or service can also be helpful to you. For example, a snapshot of your kids, your dog, or your cat can be simple and effective tools for establishing rapport and camaraderie with customers. A photo of you with that big fish you caught last summer, your boat, your airplane, or

whatever . . . pictures such as these can give you an opportunity to establish points of shared interest with your customers. Personal photographs can allow you to approach prospects on a less formal, more friendly level.

4. Everyone likes to have his or her picture taken. I have always known this and used this basic truth to good effect. I take pictures of my prospects and customers in their places of business frequently. This gives them a good feeling about me and what we're doing together. It is also very advantageous for me to have that photo with me later, when I come back to ask for a reorder or leads.

5. You will flatter your customer if you ask for permission to take "before and after" photos. It demonstrates your confidence in your product or service and is flattering to the customer's ego. It also helps reinforce in the customer's mind the idea that his or her place of business will be significantly different after your product or service is put into place.

YOUR COMPANY'S MAGAZINE AND OTHER LITERATURE

Material such as this can be particularly helpful if it contains an article or feature about you. Keep in mind the fact that everyone enjoys doing business with a celebrity. If you have earned any recognition or won awards from your company, don't be modest about it . . . use this information to let your customers know what a true professional you are!

Every company should try to provide *individualized recognition* for its salespeople. The salespeople should then learn to use that personal recognition to their maximum advantage in selling situations.

A STEEL TAPE RULER

Carry a steel tape ruler with you, and use it whenever you can. Even if you have no direct need for this type of ruler, it can still be a wonderful prop that you can use to engage your audience and hold their attention. It is very difficult to take your eyes off of a person who's talking to you while holding a steel tape extended into the air, or who's tapping the ceiling with it!

It is amazing how useful a steel tape can be in many selling situations. It is also amazing how much attention you can command by using it suddenly.

MONEY

Here's another psychological truth that few salespeople know about, and even fewer use to their advantage: If your customer sees that *you* have a lot of money, *he or she* will feel prosperous. When customers actually *see* your money, they know they are dealing with someone who should be taken seriously.

1. There are many useful techniques for building this sense of success in your customer's mind. For example, you could staple to your contract a discount for your customer in the form of cash or a check, and take it with you. In this way, the customer sees some of the advantages he'll be getting right from the start—a great way to begin any sales relationship!·

2. If you display a lot of money during a sale, you will most definitely win the customer's attention. We are all programmed to pay attention to money, and you can make that "natural programming" work for you.

3. Your customers will be more inclined to believe you aren't just interested in making money off of them if they see you already have some. Try to adopt an air of prosperity at all times!

MAPS

1. Maps, like pictures, help clarify things. It's far easier

to point out a location on a map than it is to verbally explain where it is.

2. Having maps to show your prospects or customers gives you credibility. They make you look like a busy traveling salesperson.

A POINTER

You will always look important if you pull out a pointer to indicate specific items on any graphics you may have or your sample. Like the steel tape ruler mentioned earlier, a pointer is an excellent device for gaining the attention of your audience. The pointer also tends to add a sense of importance to your statements.

HIGHLIGHTERS

Use highlighting markers freely to draw attention to the important points of your proposal, your brochures, or any other written material. Highlight printed information before you make a significant verbal statement. This adds emphasis to that point, and reinforces the information in the customer's mind.

YOUR AUTOMOBILE

If you are a traveling salesperson, you already realize that your car is an indispensable selling tool. However, you may not have realized that you can also use it as a helpful prop. I remember well how I used to pull up to the front door of a customer's location in my big Lincoln Continental Mark Five. I made sure that I gave everyone the impression that the *QEII* was pulling into a berth! Before I'd said even a single word, I'd already impressed my prospect and established in his mind that he would be dealing with a successful sales professional.

JEWELRY

Wearing expensive jewelry is another way to enhance your image and give you a special level of credibility. It gives you an air of confidence as nothing else can. It is also be a great way to start up a conversation with a prospect who notices your sparkling finery!

BUSINESS CARDS

You may think this strange, but I never give my customers my own business cards. Why? Because I consider asking for a business card to be a form of "brush-off," a way for customers to end a conversation while appearing to be polite about it. I do, however, show my customers the business card of the person who gave me their name and sent me to see them. I also show them the business cards of my other happy customers. This kind of "evidence" invariably has more impact with the customer than merely saying that this person sent me or was happy with my service.

A PEN OR PENCIL AND A PAD OF PAPER

Have you ever found yourself at a loss for words right in the middle of a presentation . . . just "gone blank" for a moment, unable to decide what to say or do next? It happens to all of us sometimes, but here's a trick to help you out of that situation with style. When you need time to think, pull out a pen or pencil and start jotting some figures onto a sheet of paper. Even if you're only stalling for time, your customers will think that you're busily working out a complex problem. You will seem far more intelligent than you would if you simply stood there, staring out into space, trying to decide what to say next!

COMPANY-RELATED ITEMS

Items such as pins, badges, jackets, coffee mugs, or anything with your company logo on it can be valuable tools.

Especially helpful are any items you may have won in a sales contest such as a ring, watch, or other items with your company's logo on it. Here again, you can reinforce in your customer's mind that he is dealing not only with a professional, but with a winner—a salesperson who has proven himself to be one of the best among his peers. This lets your prospect feel good about himself, knowing that he's doing business with a proven "A Team" sales professional.

REMEMBER . . . EVERY SELLING SITUATION IS DIFFERENT!

I hope that this lesson on tools of the trade motivates you to look carefully at your situation and decide which props you can incorporate into your presentation to make you more effective. You've probably often heard the old saying that football is a "game of inches." Well, selling is similar. We need every advantage we can get. It's up to you to find out what those advantages are, and go after them.

True professionals in every field seek out and use every advantage they can uncover. Mastering the tools you have at your disposal will inevitably give you an advantage in the extremely competitive business of selling!

How to Conduct Yourself
in the Field

How you initially conduct yourself in the field will have a profound effect on your long-term success. Many salespeople make a critical mistake early in their career that adversely affects them and their performance for a long time. Their simple mistake is holding back. They don't exert themselves to the maximum, allowing other salespeople to set the performance benchmark on the job.

That kind of passivity is tragic, because the salesperson who indulges in it lets a tremendous opportunity to slip through his fingers. A little-known truth about selling careers is that you can usually get further ahead by working hard in the first few weeks or months on the job than you ever will at any other time in that job. With hard work and preparation, you can jump out of the gate and move ahead of your peers while they're still standing at the starting line, waiting to see what will happen next.

Remember that managers eagerly watch their new recruits to see which of them has the potential for growth to a management position in the future. They also want to identify which new reps will be worth an investment of their time and money. All of these are sound reasons why hard work, self-discipline, and planning will pay off more handsomely for you at the start of a sales job than at *any* other time.

Principles

1. Your customers may occasionally evaluate you on the basis of superficialities such as your age, gender, or race. Bear in mind that those externals will never be the decisive factors that cause them to buy or not buy from you. The only reason why customers ever buy anything are value and benefits.

2. An age-old truth about selling: Every personal liability can be turned into an asset. But by the same token, any asset can, if not handled properly, become a liability.

3. The greatest attribute a salesperson can possess is not a great personality or a glib tongue but self-confidence— the assurance that he has the right product at the right price for the customer, and he's ready to do business today!

4. You obtain self-confidence through study, practice, experience, and success. The more success you experience, the more self-confident you will become.

5. The old saying "you never get a second chance to make a good first impression" holds absolutely true for all salespeople. The first impression a salesperson makes on a prospective customer is vitally important. True professionals introduce themselves with confidence. They know exactly what they are going to say and do. They expect others to listen to them.

6. A glib tongue is the worst speech impediment that a salesperson can have.

7. Always be serious and professional about the way you introduce yourself and the product or service you are selling. Customers tend to assume that you, your products, and your proposal are only as important as you indicate they are.

8. Be sure to listen to your customers at every stage in the sales process. They will usually tell you everything you need to know in order to complete a sale.

9. Remember that whenever customers agree to listen to your presentation, they are telling you that they want to

be sold, expect to be sold, and deserve to be sold. If, in the end, they are notsold, you must ask yourself a hard question: "What did I do to change my customer's mind and convince him or her not to buy today after all?"

10. When a customer shows hospitality by offering you something such as coffee, cookies, or even assistance of some kind, be sure to accept it. One of the best ways for you to ingratiate yourself with a prospective customer is to let him or her do you a favor.

11. As we noted earlier, customers will be more willing to listen to you if you look important, rich, and professional . . . but in the end, they will only buy from you if, in their minds, the value of the product or service you are offering exceeds the price you are asking.

12. Customers always appreciate straight talk. Don't ever try to trick them; inform them. Don't try to manipulate them; build value. Whenever you trick a customer into saying yes on insignificant points, all you really do is trick yourself. You set your customer up to say no at the time when it really counts.

13. Never try to "sell yourself" in order to sell the product or service you have to offer. Make your customers want your product or service so badly that they will try to please you to get a better deal.

14. When you try to sell yourself, you usually wind up as a bland, washed-out, uninteresting salesperson who isn't likely to impress anyone.

15. Don't "accommodate" your customers by trying to find a time when it might be convenient for them to buy. Create a selling situation in which it is always to your customer's advantage to buy now.

16. Don't limit your potential by telling customers that you're willing to wait until they are ready and able to pay for your product or service. Create so much value and urgency that they will rearrange their priorities to come up with the money here and now.

17. Never isolate your customer from his or her business, family, or friends out of fear that these "distractions" will disrupt your presentation. Welcome any distractions you encounter, and turn them to your advantage. Your prospect's customers, family, and friends will often help you by encouraging the customer to buy. After all, bystanders can afford to be big spenders. Your product or service won't cost them any money!

18. Don't attempt to make sales to your family, friends, or members of your church, club, or lodge. Don't capitalize on your personal relationships. Sell your product or service based only on the merits it has to offer, and on your ability to sell.

19. Don't bore your customers. Tell them only what they need to know about such matters as construction and features. Then, spend most of your time selling value and benefits.

20. Never lower your price in the hope that this reduction, in and of itself, will make the sale for you. Lower your price only when it helps your customer buy something now that he would otherwise wait to buy at a later time.

21. Remember that every time you lower your price, you also lower the value of your product or service in the mind of your customer.

22. Don't try to get your customers to agree with you on the points you make. One sure mark of an amateur is his or her constant need for reassurance or approval. A professional, on the other hand, is able to state a position clearly, with no concern one way or the other whether the customer agrees.

23. The best time to call on customers is when they are busy. Whenever customers are busy handling their own business, serving customers, and earning money, they feel prosperous. It naturally follows that when they feel prosperous, they are much more likely to buy.

24. Calling on your customers when they're busy lends a special sense of importance to your visit. Work to convince your customers that what you have to say to them is so important that they should make the time to listen to you. When you do this, you establish a foundation of value on which you can build toward the final sale. When your customers are busy, it adds an air of urgency to your offer. A well-crafted, carefully practiced presentation should always be more interesting than any distractions that might occur in your customer's place of business.

25. I believe that if my sales presentation is not more exciting than any distraction that may arise, then I don't deserve to make the sale.

26. We will always interrupt our schedule when we have to deal with something that's more important than our schedule. The more important the matter, the more justification we have for the interruption. In the same way, when our schedule is interrupted, we place more importance on whatever it is that causes the interruption. If you successfully interrupt your customer's important schedule to show him your product or service, it places a higher psychological premium on the value of that product or service.

27. When people are unable to manage their time effectively, they are always behind schedule . . . no matter how much or how little work they have to do.

28. If people cannot manage themselves, they will always fail, no matter how much talent they have.

29. When people are unable to manage their money, they will always be broke no matter how much they earn.

30. Sell with confidence. When a good salesperson walks into a room, the customer should hear something clanging together . . . and it shouldn't be a set of car keys!

31. All the world's a stage, and salespeople get most of the best parts in the show.

32. You don't let your barber pick the stocks in which

you'll invest. You don't let your brother-in-law fix your car. In the same way, don't let anybody who has never sold tell you anything about how to sell.

33. With a lot of practice, study, and effort, anyone can become good at sales.

34. The difference in effort between being good and being great is really only about 10 percent or less.

35. If a good salesperson is willing to work 20 percent harder than a great salesperson, no one will be able to beat him.

36. You know customers are buying when they start trying to convince you that they can help you make future sales.

37. Always remember that silent partners won't remain silent when it comes time to write a check.

38. Don't ever sell your customer more than you know he can afford to buy. That's bad business for both of you.

39. The best students usually become the best teachers. The best followers usually become the best leaders.

40. I'm often accused of analyzing things too closely. I like to find small problems and then correct them. Always be as meticulous as you can.

41. The secret of enjoyment is to first develop an appetite and then satisfy it. It's the variety that leads to the pleasure. Continual gratification would be every bit as unpleasant and destructive as continual deprivation.

42. If you must make a mistake, be sure to make it in favor of your salespeople. If you always demonstrate a genuine concern for your salespeople, you will have loyal and conscientious workers.

43. People are more important than any material goods. Never value products, merchandise, money, machines, or any other things more highly than you value the feelings and the wellbeing of the people who work for you.

44. A truth worth remembering: All products and services are worthless without salespeople to sell them.

45. Try to be friendly, live in peace, and treat people well. The only thing that should ever anger you in your professional life is the mistreatment of your salespeople, not any slight or mistreatment that you yourself might experience.

46. This quotation captures the essence of why I've achieved my goals: "My strength lies solely in my tenacity." (Louis Pasteur)

47. It is always better to be respected than to be liked.

48. Don't be distracted by criticism. Remember the old adage, "The dog barks, but the caravan moves on."

49. "It is not what you give, but what you share, for a gift without a giver is bare." (The Vision of Sir Launfal, James Russell Lowell)

50. Amateurs and peddlers rely on their personalities and their glib tongues. Professionals rely on practice, sound principles, and hard work.

SELLING YOURSELF BEFORE YOU SELL YOUR PRODUCT OR SERVICE

Many misconceptions can cause salespeople to work below their capabilities. Selling yourself before you sell your product or service is one of the worst. The clever person who first came up with this idea has probably ruined more sales careers than any other person, except for the one who said, "Success comes from a positive mental attitude." Selling yourself is not only degrading, but it doesn't work. Selling yourself before you sell your product or service is exactly what it sounds like—a sellout. A salesperson needs all the self-confidence and individuality he or she can muster. The reason people like to talk to and do business with a salesperson is because of the self-confidence and individuality of the salesperson. When you try to sell yourself, you stand a good chance of destroying your self-confidence and your individuality.

Principles

1. Your customers want to do business with a professional, someone who takes pride in his or her work. The concept of "selling yourself" implies accommodation, compliance, and a compromise of your own individuality.

2. Preserve your individuality and dignity by conducting yourself with pride, self-confidence, and professionalism at all times.

3. Sell your product with pride, self-confidence, and professionalism. Make your customer want your product or service so badly that *he feels* compelled to accommodate *you!*

4. Great salespeople always maintain their unique opinions and personality. They make their customers *want* their product or service so badly that those customers feel compelled to accommodate the salesperson by *buying.*

5. Remember, people will never buy from you just because they like you—at least, they'll never buy anything more important than Girl Scout cookies! Your customers will only buy because they like what you are selling.

6. No truly professional salesperson would ever want his customers to buy only because they like him. You don't want to wind up like Willy Loman, do you?

7. When you're constantly selling yourself, you wind up as little more than a generic, uninteresting, washed-out salesperson without a distinct personality. Even if this tactic worked—which it doesn't—why would you want to pay such a high price to make your living?

8. It boils down to this: "Selling yourself" is exactly what it sounds like . . . a form of prostitution.

9. I could not possibly sell myself for one simple reason: I have such a high opinion of my worth that no one could ever afford me!

Managing Your Finances

All too often, people who might have enjoyed a brilliant career in sales wind up as failures only because they never learned how to manage their finances properly. Similarly, people who make an above-average income in sales often don't do well financially because they can't manage their money well. Perhaps the most common mistake that salespeople make is failing to realize that selling always has its financial ups and downs. Misguided salespeople will spend their money when it is abundant, as if the good times were going to last forever. Then when they encounter a dry spell, they can't handle the financial obligations they have assumed.

Principles

1. The second most common reason why good salespeople fail in this profession, especially in commission sales, is because they are unable to manage their finances properly.

2. Wise salespeople are misers until they become firmly established in their profession. Then, once they become established, these salespeople find themselves financially well off.

3. Invest in our profession. Use your money to buy

good clothes, a decent car, and a high-quality briefcase to enhance your professional image and self-confidence.

4. Understand and accept the fact that selling will always be a "feast or famine" business. Be sure to keep much of what you earn during the "feast" times to help see you through the inevitable "famines" to come. For salespeople, having money in the bank is just as important as having inventory in the store is for businesspeople.

5. Be sure always to make your income-tax payments on time. Failure to do this is a critical mistake that many new salespeople make.

6. Make it a point to save at least 10 percent of your income. This is how you pay yourself first. Don't wait until you start making a lot of money to set something aside for yourself. Start now, and keep it up.

7. I repeat . . . when people are incapable of managing their money, they will always be broke, no matter how much they make.

8. Admitting that you are wrong is the first step in correcting your mistakes.

9. You will never be able to pull others out of a ditch unless you remain on solid ground. Keep yourself financially sound so that you can help others who "slip off the road" now and then.

10. The good Samaritan would have been worthless if he had not had enough money to help out the poor man who had been robbed.

11. Some wise advice from my grandma: "Get all you can, and can all you get!"

12. Salespeople, think of this point before you squander or mismanage your finances: Your first obligation is always to the wellbeing of your family. Your professional success will not mean much if your family is neglected and fails in the process. By the same token, your family must also understand that your success depends on their support.

13. Commission salespeople should realize that for all practical purposes, they own their own business and have sole responsibility for its success or failure. As such, they must understand that starting up any new business always calls for financial sacrifice.

14. Commission salespeople must be prepared to go it alone. They must be their own commissaries. They must store away the resources that come in during the feast to carry them through the famine to come.

15. When you find yourself in a hole, quit digging.

Personal Integrity

Personal integrity is one of the rarest and most precious qualities a salesperson can possess. Even those salespeople who have little integrity of their own will admit that they admire those who have it. In the sales profession, much is often made of those who are clever, but honesty will always have much more impact on your overall success.

A salesperson has the opportunity to make deals and influence customers to a much higher degree than most other professionals. For this reason, their integrity, or lack of it, has the potential to do great good or harm. The most important aspect of integrity is that it affects the person with whom you will live most intimately for the rest of your life . . . yourself.

Principles

1. Never use any sales tactic that might compromise your personal integrity.

2. Never denigrate your competition. Strong, confident, and mature salespeople can afford to be magnanimous toward their professional competitors.

3. Always maintain higher ethical standards than you expect from others. Always set a higher ethical standard than your competition.

4. We should never think evil of a person until he has done us at *least* as many bad turns as good turns.

5. Telling customers at the beginning of your pitch that you are not a salesperson in order to set them at ease and gain an alliance is an unethical practice. It begins your relationship with a lie. It also implies that you believe there's something shameful about the profession of selling. Never do it!

6. If you derive your income from the sale of a product or service, then you are, by definition, a salesperson. To say otherwise is simply dishonest.

7. Professional salespeople, like all other professionals, should take pride in their occupation.

8. Everyone wants to do business with a real professional. Your customers are just the same. They all want to do business with a professional salesperson . . . and that person is *you*, right?

9. If you are unable to take pride in being a professional salesperson, then you are in the wrong profession. Do yourself and the sales profession a favor, and find yourself another occupation.

10. High ethical principles promote self-confidence. When you know you are "playing it straight," you spend your energy focusing on your customer's needs and your ability to meet those needs . . . not what your next manipulative "trick" is going to be. And as any successful salesperson will tell you, self-confidence is a major quality needed for success in sales.

SOME SPECIAL THOUGHTS FOR SALES MANAGERS

11. How do you ever expect to instill pride in the young salespeople who work for you if you teach them to tell their customers that they are not salespeople? When you do this, you have taught them to lie to their customers about their profession!

12. How can you ever expect to instill confidence in your salespeople's customers when it quickly becomes evident to them that you've told your salespeople to lie simply to gain an audience?

13. Remember the old maxim: If a person will steal *for* you, he will also steal *from* you. Many sales organizations and managers teach their dealers to use shady tactics, but later on, they are amazed when they become crooks, stealing from both their customers and their company.

14. Delayed reprimands are often ineffective or even counterproductive. If you, as a manager, allow any of your salespeople to get away with improper behavior for any length of time, they will come to believe they can always get away with it. Whenever a reprimand becomes necessary, deliver it immediately.

15. We all tend to use two different rulers when we measure people. We have a short and flexible ruler to measure ourselves and a long and rigid one to measure others. We would be much better off it we were to reverse those rulers, and judge only ourselves by the tougher standard.

16. People tend to judge others by their actions, but judge themselves by their motives. Be harder on yourself, and give others the benefit of the doubt.

17. You cannot make an intelligent judgment about an ethical question that arises within yours sales force until you hear both sides of the story. Make sure you talk to both the customer *and* the salesperson before you form any decisions.

Seizing the Prize

Just about everyone likes to win prizes, and I'm no exception. A couple of rooms in my home are filled with trophies, plaques, awards, and other memorabilia that I've won in sales contests over the years. These prizes gave me great pleasure when I first won them, and they continue to give me pleasure when I look at them now and relive in my mind the victories and successes they represent.

But I don't just love prizes . . . I also love to *win*. Whenever I encounter a top ten list, I want to be number one. I have often been told that I'm competitive to a fault! I also love it when I am underestimated by my competition. I get a real kick out of letting people convince themselves that I have no chance to win, and then watching the look on their faces when I come on like gangbusters to take the big prize. Still, none of this is all that unusual. Think about it . . . don't you like to win? Of course you do!

The truth is, everybody likes to win! Everyone in your organization would love to be the top salesperson if he or she could only figure out how to achieve that goal. Think about everything that could come your way if you were the top salesperson in your company. You would gain:

Money. You'd have all the money you would ever need.

Fame. Everyone would know who you are and what you have accomplished.

Influence. Everyone listens to the opinions of a top producer because he or she always gets the job done.

Self-esteem. You would feel really good about yourself.

Respect. Everyone from the top management of your company to your peers and even your competition would hold you in high regard.

Let me ask you this important question: *What do you think is the most important characteristic any person should have in order to become a top salesperson?* Take a moment now to write down your answer or answers. You'll find my answer near the end of this chapter.

There's an ancient myth that tells the story of a sad character named Ezirp. This poor man was doomed to roll a large boulder up to the top of a hill. Unfortunately, he was never quite able to reach his goal. He would roll the boulder as far as he could, and then he would stop. As Ezirp was catching his breath, the boulder would roll back down the hill, and he would have to begin his task all over again. Ezirp was a hard worker. He showed up for his job every day. He always did what he was told to do. However, he was never quite able to achieve his goal. He was the victim of a curse that prevented him from ever attaining his objective.

Many salespeople suffer from the effects of a similar curse. It's the curse of *mediocrity.* It is the curse of failing to follow through and win.

ARE YOU CURSED LIKE EZIRP?

Are you going through your life doing only what's needed to get by, but never pushing yourself to reach the top?

Are you always thinking about accomplishing your goals someday, but never taking action to realize them?

What would happen to you if, just once, you exerted yourself, and took real control of your finances?

What would happen if you stuck with it and pulled yourself completely out of debt?

What would your life be like if you worked until you had a large bankroll of cash available to you for your exclusive use?

What would happen if you studied and practiced until you knew your presentation completely and were able to deliver it convincingly?

What if you worked hard enough to become the top salesperson or top manager in your company?

What if, just once, you worked as hard as you could and found out just how good you could really be?

I'm sure you already know the answer to all of these questions . . . *it could and would change your life!*

Scientific researchers tell us that it's almost impossible for an athlete to win a marathon without experiencing what's called the "second effort." What is this effort? It is really just a change in *mental attitude*. Most people don't realize what they're really capable of achieving because they never exert themselves hard enough to test their capabilities. It is only when salespeople commit themselves to reaching down into those unknown and untapped resources inside themselves, and demand more of themselves than they ever thought they could give, that their true potential is finally revealed. This means doing the best you can until you think you can do no more . . . and then doing still more. *That* is the essence of "seizing the prize," and it could change your life forever.

Most salespeople think that if their external circumstances could be changed, they would then change their behavior. This common belief is not true. In fact, it is a reversal of the truth. In order for people to change their circumstances, they must first change their direction, focus, and motivation. You can take a pig out of the mud, wash him up, put a bow tie on him, polish his nails, and put him behind the wheel of a Cadillac . . . but he'll still be a pig. When the first opportunity presents itself, that pig will find another mudhole and return to his piggy ways. Now, I don't want to offend anyone, but no matter how a person's external circumstances might change, that person will not change. If, however, people work to change their direction, focus, and motivation, they will then be able to change their circumstances.

I believe that the most important attributes leading to success in professional sales . . . or any field . . . are decision making, action, preparation, determination, and hard work. If you just change the way you think about yourself, you can change the world! Consider the following examples.

Charlemagne. He conquered the world and founded the Holy Roman Empire because he believed he could do it. If you let history be your guide, you will learn that behind every great event, every great movement, and every great stride forward for mankind, there was a man or woman whose changed attitude changed the world.

Joan of Arc. She was a farm girl who firmly believed that she had been called to lead her nation to victory. She was no smarter, taller, tougher, or richer than any other French farm girl. She simply started to think differently about herself. She had a firm conviction in the truth of her beliefs. Her conviction and faith in herself were so powerful that they gave her the ability to convince others and change their attitudes. Joan did not inherit a fortune, win the lottery, or become a queen. She changed her attitude, changed her actions, and then changed a nation.

Vladimir Ilyich Ulyanov (Lenin). His ideas, though now proven incorrect, were adopted by half of mankind. Why? Because he believed in them fervently. The world will almost always follow someone who believes strongly and convincingly in himself and his ideas. You can say what you want about the boy, but right or wrong, his changed attitude changed the world for over seventy years, and the legacy he has left behind will affect the world for generations to come.

How would it change your life if you decided to do whatever it took to be the top salesperson in your organization for one month? Now, I don't mean being the top salesperson for any *given* month. I mean becoming the top salesperson in your organization for any month ever! Why don't you make it your personal goal to set a record in your sales organization for monthly sales?

Imagine that for one month, you decided to give up "partying" and goofing off. Imagine that you decided that for one month, you would not even rest. You would simply work and sleep and then work some more until you set a new sales record for your company. You would dedicate yourself to doing more than anyone else in your company had ever done.

Does that sound like a tough challenge? Well, I did it once when I was a field salesperson. I put out as much effort in one day as I usually did in two, and I kept that pace up for a full month. Believe me, this was no easy task. I had always worked hard and put in long hours, so adding to that burden was a challenge. As I see it now, if I could double my output for a short time, as I did in those days, then anyone can do it. When I had finished, I'd set a one-month sales record with the company that stands to this day. It has remained now for over twenty years! You can do something like this, too . . . if you are willing to work hard enough.

By the way, here's my answer to the question I posed at the beginning of this chapter. The most important characteristic any person should have in order to become a top salesperson is *determination*. The person who refuses to accept defeat will always be a winner! If you can muster up enough determination, you will ultimately acquire all the other characteristics you'll ever need to be a success.

If you got that right, you get an Ezirp, which, as you've no doubt already figured out, is *Prize* spelled backwards. (By the way, as you may also know, the person who rolled the huge stone up the hill was really a character from Greek mythology named Sisyphus.)

Now, how do you successfully develop a positive mental attitude that will produce determination? I mean a *real* positive mental attitude—not some phony, hyped-up, temporary, and meaningless euphoria that is so popular with the charlatans of salesmanship practicing today. The best way to develop a positive attitude is to take *positive physical action.* There's magic and power in action. All human success depends to a great extent on action.

If you aren't sure how to get yourself started, consider the following list of practical action steps for beginning on the road to real sale success.

1. Decide what you want so badly that you will do whatever it takes to get it. Define your goal as clearly as possible. If you can, quantify your goal. (For example, "I will make X dollars in new paid sales.") The clearer your goal, the more likely you are to achieve it. It is very difficult to focus your energies on a vague target.

2. Develop a strategy to obtain your goal. Then, write down what you have to do to achieve the goal. Be sure to list each step in your strategy. This "action plan" will be your roadmap that will guide you from where you are now to where you want to be.

3. Set a time limit for yourself. Decide *when* you want to achieve your goal. An action plan without a timeframe usually deteriorates into a worthless wish list after a short while.

4. Start working. Take action. Do whatever you can do to get yourself started. And don't kid yourself . . . there is *always* something you can do, no matter how small, to get you through that first door. Once you're under way, you'll see that the first door you open will lead to other doors, and they will lead to still others, and eventually they will lead to success.

5. Work consistently until you have achieved your goal. Work however hard you have to work. Work however many hours, days, weeks, or months you have to work.

6. Don't allow yourself to be sidetracked, discouraged, or defeated. Remember that no matter how hard you may think you have it, other salespeople have put up with a lot

more than you have, and still made it. Don't ever quit. Stick with it until you succeed. Don't quit, don't quit, don't quit!

7. Motivate yourself with your principles, not with your feelings. Do what you do because you have the character to do it. Remember that your feelings change . . . they are an unreliable motivator. Principles are constant. They are dependable, and do not change with time, trends, or attitudes. Let your principles be your guide.

Rest assured that when you achieve your goal, you will most *certainly* develop a positive mental attitude! You will be filled with that adrenaline and good feeling reserved for true winners.

Professionally Speaking

Salespeople make their living with their speaking ability. To a large degree, the more effectively a salesperson speaks, the more money he or she will earn.

There is usually a dramatic difference between what a professional speaker earns as a salesperson and what an amateur speaker earns. Improving the way you speak can make a big difference in your income.

Think with me about this for a moment. Most salespeople say basically the same things about their product or service. But despite this, one salesperson is able to make thousands of dollars every week. Another salesperson who sells the same product or service and says essentially the same things about it can barely make his car payments.

Transforming yourself from an amateur speaker into a professional speaker will make a big difference in your income. Let's make that transition as soon as possible! As with all worthwhile changes in life, it starts with the *decision* to change. Then comes a plan, then action, then hard work, practice, and determination to reach your goal.

The following are a few helpful points to remember as you begin making your own transition from amateur speaker to professional speaker.

1. Amateurs learn their presentation adequately, and

then settle into a career of repetitive mediocrity.

2. Professionals learn their presentation *perfectly* and then master its delivery. They not only know what to say, but also why they are saying it. They study the background material that relates to all the points in their presentation. They master every word, gesture, and voice inflection in their presentation for effectiveness. They spend many long hours practicing what they're going to say and how they will say it. They practice in front of their managers and peers. They practice in front of their spouse and in front of themselves using a mirror. A professional speaker thinks of him- or herself as an actor who masters eye contact, gestures, movements, and voice inflection.

3. Amateurs do not make their points clearly. They do not think through what they want to say ahead of time, or decide on the best way to say it. That is one reason why it is so important to stick to a prepared presentation. In sales, there is usually no better way to convey the message you want to get across than to follow your company's presentation.

4. Professionals make their points clearly because they know *exactly* what they want to say, and they plan ahead to determine the best way to say it. They thoroughly master the content and delivery of their presentation.

5. Amateurs "overexplain" their points. They use too many illustrations, and they repeat themselves. They are not confident of their ability to make their points clearly, so they talk too much and often make themselves harder to understand. In their futile attempts to make themselves clear, they become confusing, and lose the attention of their customer.

6. Professionals do not overexplain. They make their points clearly, then stop talking, or move ahead to the next point. They are completely confident that they have been understood. They also observe their customer and are able to determine if that customer has understood what has been said.

7. Amateurs do not pause between sentences or the points they make. They run their sentences together in an effort to close out any interruptions. In their insecurity, they believe that if the other person speaks, they won't be able to finish their thoughts. When their customers do speak, they do not listen. Instead, they are busy thinking about what they are going to say next.

8. Professionals use pauses in their presentation for great dramatic effect. They are confident that their message is so interesting and informative that the customer wants them to keep speaking.

9. Amateurs get too physically close to their customers in order to hold their attention. In fact, one of the easiest ways to identify an amateur speaker is that he wants to get a little closer to you than you think is appropriate. As you already know, having someone crowd in on you while he talks is both disconcerting and annoying. It certainly is not a way to win a customer over in a selling situation.

10. Professionals are wise enough to stand back and address their customers from an appropriate distance. They know that if they are interesting and informative, their customer will decide to move closer to them if it helps them see or hear better. Professional speakers want to stand back to talk to as many people at one time as possible, even when there is only one customer present.

11. Amateurs try to get agreement on their various points and opinions as they speak. They seek assurance from their customer by asking approval and using weak words like okay. It is not helpful "as is commonly taught" to get approval on small points in order to get approval on a big point. This tactic only shows your uncertainty.

12. Professionals do not seek or need anyone's approval. They state their case in a positive, logical, and confident manner, and expect that their presentation will be met with approval based on its own merit.

13. Amateurs are constantly trying to prove or verify what they say. They are unsure about their ability to tell a

convincing story. They use documentation and the testimony of others to prove their case or reinforce their truthfulness. While it may at times be appropriate to use documentation to prove your point, its often merely illustrates your own insecurity.

14. Professionals expect to be believed. They do not depend on documentation or verification to prove that what they say is true or valid. They speak from knowledge and confidence, and they expect their customers to believe what they say.

15. Amateurs try to isolate their customers because they fear outside interference or distractions.

16. Professionals don't mind distractions, because they are confident they can hold their customer's attention through any distraction. Professional salespeople like to talk to as many people as possible and then use any interruptions that come up as opportunities to illustrate their points.

17. Amateurs ask questions to try to be sociable and get their customer's attention. The questions they ask are not well thought out and are often meaningless. It soon becomes evident to the customer that the salesperson doesn't really care about his answers because he seldom listens to those answers or responds appropriately. Amateurs often go so far as to answer their own questions, or assist the customer in answering. In so doing, they get little useful information from their customer.

18. Professionals ask very specific and pertinent questions. They determine what information they need, and they ask the precise questions that will elicit that information. They listen carefully to the answers they receive and are able to use the information to their advantage. They respond appropriately to the information, showing their customer that they understand and care.

19. Amateurs ignore their environment, situation, and customers. They do not use their power of observation to help their cause. They often get themselves into difficulty

because the place they choose to sit or stand is not appropriate for giving a presentation. When the sun is in your eyes, or you have to turn your head far around to see your customer, or there is no place for you to put your materials, it is difficult to be effective.

20. Professionals are careful to observe their environment, situation, and customers as much as possible. By listening conscientiously to their customers and painstakingly observing their surroundings, they gain information that is invaluable to them in making a sale. They plan their strategy by taking full advantage of the selling environment in which they find themselves.

21. Amateurs learn how to use their props adequately. They do not understand the tremendous power available to them in the proper use of the visual aids that are a part of their "sales package."

22. Professionals master the proper use of their props. They discover and then practice the most effective techniques for using every item at their disposal. The effective use of sales props is the unmistakable mark of a selling professional. What exactly is a sales prop? As I said in a previous chapter, it can be virtually anything. Your brochure books, photos, charts and graphs, briefcase, and more are all tools that can be mastered in order to make your presentation more engaging and effective. One of the best ways to master your props is to practice by "role playing" your presentation with your sales peers as you each critically observe one another.

23. Amateurs hope their customers will listen to them and then comply with their proposal. This attitude is where the silly notion that "selling is a numbers game" got its start.

24. Professionals *expect* their customers to listen to them and then buy into their proposal. One of the most important attributes that any salesperson can possess is self-confidence. You should deliver your message confidently and expect your customer to comply.

25. Amateurs hear many objections. They fear and overreact to these. They also believe that overcoming the customer's objections will result in a sale.

26. Professionals hear very few objections. They welcome objections, and only address an objection when it is in their own best interest to do so. They know that the objection usually has little to do with the sale. They don't hear many objections because they think ahead and structure their presentation in such a way that it stops most objections and answers others before they arise. They welcome objections because they've thought out answers that will turn the objection to their advantage. They don't overreact to objections because they are confident of their ability to deal with any situation. They know that most objections are born of the customer's insecurity and lack of information but enhanced by the salesperson's insecurity and ineptitude. Truly professional salespeople know that only value sells, not overcoming objections.

27. Amateurs *look* like amateurs and dress like amateurs. Looking like a loser is a handicap that no salesperson can afford.

28. Professionals look like professionals and dress like professionals. It is a simple fact of life that people listen to important-looking and important-sounding people.

29. An amateur acts like an amateur, conducts himself in amateurish ways, and is treated like an amateur. He expects to be treated like an amateur. As a result, he is also paid like an amateur.

30. A professional acts like a professional and conducts himself like a professional. These people are treated like professionals and expect to be treated like professionals. They display confidence, knowledge, pride, and enthusiasm. These are the highly paid professionals whom so many people in other careers envy.

31. Amateurs look for easy sales. They "cherry-pick" and look only for obvious needs. They try to capitalize on

their relationships with their family, church, and friends to make sales. They overemphasize the importance of leads and the recommendations of others.

32. Professionals look for a challenge. They create needs in the minds of their customers and then fill those needs. They do not want charity and therefore never depend on selling to friends, family, or church members. They have the confidence that they can sell their product to any qualified buyer if they are given a chance.

Think with me for a moment. Arnold Palmer doesn't play miniature golf. He looks for a challenging golf course. As a professional salesperson, you should prepare yourself for a real challenge and look for it.

Each of these points deserves more elaboration and thought. As with anything worthwhile, becoming a professional speaker and salesperson requires a lot of effort. Of course, there are many other attributes that distinguish the professional salesperson. Perhaps this lesson will start some salesperson thinking in terms of becoming more professional. I hope so!

The Sales Presentation

The most important thing I can say to any new salesperson is to *absolutely master your sales presentation*. Learn to say it perfectly, learn to say it convincingly, and learn to say it immediately.

The second most important thing I can say to a new salesperson is to stay on your sales presentation. It is the sales presentation that sells the product. If you add to it, take away from it, or get off track with it, you will be less successful . . . guaranteed.

The third important piece of advice I would give to a new salesperson is to deliver your sales presentation *often*. Nothing will help you succeed like the confidence you get from delivering your presentation to a customer. The most important factor in my own success as a sales manager was to evaluate the sales presentations my dealers made on a regular basis. Getting the dealers back on track with their presentations did more to boost volume than any contest I ever instituted.

1. Why do salespeople have presentations? They have a lot of information to offer customers in a relatively short period of time. If customers don't understand the proposal, they will not buy what is offered . . . or they will cancel their order later. The presentation is designed to sell the product or service in the most persuasive manner possible. Anyone

can become a successful salesperson if he or she learns the presentation and uses it properly.

2. Learning the presentation is one of the most important keys to becoming successful in our business. However, merely reciting the script of a presentation is not enough. It is essential that presentations be given clearly, convincingly, enthusiastically . . . and constantly!

3. If you yourself are convinced of the truth of what you are saying, you will be convincing to your customers.

4. Rehearse and practice your presentation in the same way that Redford or Streisand rehearse and practice for the roles they play.

5. Much of the value, and most of the urgency, is already built into your company's standard sales presentation. The delivery of the presentation is also your best opportunity to build rapport with the customer. Always keep that in mind, and never allow yourself to become condescending or boring!

6. Say what you have to say with confidence, pride, and excitement. When you do, you can't help but be more effective.

7. Every good sales presentation includes three fundamental elements:

a. *Value.* The presentation builds enough value into the product or service to motivate the customer to make a positive buying decision.

b. *Urgency.* The presentation gives the customer a logical reason to buy *now.*

c. *Clarity.* The presentation tells customers everything they need to know about the product or service so they can make an intelligent decision about whether or not to buy.

8. Three basic elements must always be present when you build a fire. They are fuel, heat, and oxygen. As with fire, three basic elements must also be present when you want to make a successful sale. They are value, urgency, and clarity.

9. All salespeople should have their managers evaluate

both their presentation and their "close" on a regular basis. When this evaluation is completed, the manager should make sure the salesperson omits whatever has been added, restores whatever has been forgotten or left out, and does whatever else is necessary to make the presentation clear, exciting, and convincing.

10. Become an actor . . . a *great* actor. Learn your lines, choreograph your movements, and focus your entire performance on your single, overriding objective: to sell the customer.

11. The longer I work in sales, the more I realize the real importance of clarity. I'm firmly convinced that most salespeople could increase their sales by 20 to 50 percent if they made sure that their customers always clearly understood the proposal they were offering.

12. Keep in mind that about 50 percent of your customers will have a hard time envisioning anything from your verbal description, no matter how good you are. Be sure that any explanation you offer is graphic, clear, and well crafted.

13. Structure your proposal in a manner that will impress your customer. Be certain that he or she completely understands the offer you are making.

14. Be certain that you make your customers aware of any unique features of your product or service. Also, make sure that they fully understand any responsibilities or obligations they may be assuming when they buy.

15. Master and use every sales aid your company provides to help ensure your success.

16. Be sure that you have everything prepared ahead of time so that every presentation you make moves ahead smoothly and effortlessly.

17. Build value constantly, from the beginning to the end of your presentation. You can never overdo it.

18. Enthusiasm is contagious. You can help make your customer excited about your offer by being excited yourself.

19. Don't rush into a discussion about price. This is the telltale sign of an amateur. Remember that price will never sell a product or service until you have first built value in the mind of the customer.

20. Let your customers know that you think the offer you're making is something special and that you expect them to recognize that fact and jump on it eagerly.

21. If the customer seems lethargic, do whatever you can to make him or her move around. If that isn't possible, move around yourself. Be dramatic! Do whatever you can to get the blood and the adrenaline flowing in both of you.

22. Be very clear about what you will expect your customer to do if he or she accepts your offer. This should typically conclude with your expectation that the customer will place the order now.

23. See to it that your customer knows what he might have to pay for a similar product or service if he does not take advantage of your special offer, here and now.

24. Also, see to it that your customer knows what he or she would have to pay if you were selling your product or service under "normal" circumstances . . . that is, without the special offer you are making to this customer.

25. Make your offer with complete confidence. Ask for the order, and expect to hear a "yes" from the customer.

26. If the customer decides to accept your offer, be sure to restate and clarify any customer's objections in the transaction.

27. Remember, first, learn your presentation perfectly. Second, learn how to deliver your presentation convincingly. Third, study and analyze each part of your presentation until you know exactly what you are saying and why you are saying it.

28. Why should you use your company's standard presentation? It has been designed to present and demonstrate your product or service in the best possible light.

29. The standard presentation gives you the best possible opportunity to build value into your product or service. And of course, the perception of value is the only reason that anybody ever buys anything.

30. Your standard presentation gives you the best possible opportunity to create urgency in the selling situation. Urgency simply means giving your customer a logical reason to buy now.

31. The standard presentation gives you the best possible opportunity to prepare and set up the close of the sale.

32. Anyone, even someone with little talent or experience, can be taught to sell effectively if he will only learn his presentation perfectly and then learn how to deliver it *convincingly*.

33. A standard presentation makes it possible for experienced salespeople to teach new salespeople how to sell effectively. Growth in any sales organization is practically impossible without a standard presentation.

34. The standard presentation given to you by your company represents the accumulated experience and knowledge of many people over an extended period of time. These people have already been down the road you will soon travel. They have already learned how to sell your product or service, and they are freely willing to share with you what they've learned. By using the information they give you, you will be able to avoid the mistakes they have made, and gain from everything they have discovered or created.

35. It is unlikely that you, a newcomer, will stumble upon a better way to sell your product than your co-workers who have studied and worked for a long time and sharpened their skills based on their experience.

36. When salespeople are uncertain, unprofessional, or careless even by a factor of only 5 percent in their introduction, explanation, presentation, or close, they can reduce their sales by as much as 50 percent.

37. Most salespeople could increase their sales by 50 percent with no extra effort by simply demonstrating more professionalism in their introduction, explanation, presentation, and close.

38. Always talk slowly, listen carefully . . . and think quickly!

39. Never argue with a fool. If you do, it becomes difficult for others to tell which of you is which. I have a simple solution for handling this problem: When the customer quits making sense, I leave.

40. "The manner of your speaking is fully as important as the matter, as more people have ears to be tickled than understanding to judge." (Lord Chesterfield, 1694-1773)

41. Who was Edward Everett? On November 19, 1863, he delivered an oration at the dedication of a national cemetery in Gettysburg, Pennsylvania as a memorial to the men who had fought and died there. He spoke over two hours. When Abraham Lincoln followed Everett, he spoke for under three minutes. Everyone remembers Lincoln's address, but no one remembers a thing that Everett had to say. Perhaps we should take a lesson from Lincoln. Say what you have to say, then stop talking.

Being a Winner in Sales

Salespeople, by their very nature, like to win at just about everything. They are a competitive breed and respond to contests and challenges more readily than most people. I have had spectacular success as a salesman, and I loved the opportunity to compete with my professional peers that every new day presented to me. One of the most gratifying aspects of my career has been the trips, contests, prizes, and trophies I've won in the many sales contests I've been taken part in over the years.

There's a big difference between having talent and having the ability to *win*. Most contests are not won by the most talented participant. If you truly want to be a winner, study and apply the following principles.

1. Winning at sales is a lot like being a successful buyer at a public auction. At an auction, the person who's willing to pay the highest price always walks off with the prize. The person who wins at sales is the one who's willing to pay the highest price in hours worked, in personal commitment, in careful preparation, and in precise planning for the task at hand. Now, ask yourself this simple question. Are you willing to pay the price of winning?

2. The real difference between a winning and a losing effort is almost *always* defined by the intensity and the

duration of the effort. Losers make a halfhearted attempt to succeed and quit as soon as they confront a real challenge. Winners go at it with intensity, give it their all, and stick with it until they get what they want.

3. Without a firm decision, personal commitment, and well-defined plan to win, a salesperson will probably succeed only at losing.

4. You can achieve any objective in life if you first define your goal clearly, develop the best possible strategy for achieving your goal, and then work hard enough and long enough to achieve it.

5. Focus on your goals with all the intensity you can muster. Remember that it is *focus* that makes all the difference between the dim glow of a candle and the piercing intensity of a laser beam.

6. Organize your time. Use it wisely so you can accomplish in a single day or week what it takes your competition two days or two weeks to accomplish.

7. Winners never allow themselves the luxury of an excuse for failure. It should make you angry when you catch yourself making excuses for falling short of your goals.

8. Winners do not allow their family or friends to try to make them feel better when they fail by making excuses for them. Make sure your family knows that you don't want any excuses to lose . . . you only want a motivation to *win*.

9. Average salespeople prepare for their sales calls by doing only as much as they think they have to do to get the job done. Winners are constantly preparing themselves until they are the very best at what they do. When you achieve and sustain your "personal best," you'll always be a winner.

10. The laws of physics also apply to sales: It will take you about ten times more energy to get your sales career moving ahead as it will to keep it moving once it's on its way. You must exert intense energy to get the momentum of your life started and moving steadily forward. Then you must discipline yourself to maintain or even accelerate that momentum.

11. Most salespeople tend to work in "fits and starts." They push hard to get their momentum going, and then they slow down again. No salesperson can ever have enough energy to succeed that way.

12. As I said earlier, the number-one reason salespeople fail is because they don't work hard enough to succeed, especially when starting their new career. If you always work hard and do more than you are either asked to do or are expected to do, you will *always* be a winner.

13. We must always take the work we do very seriously and let our customers know that we are serious! But at the same time, we shouldn't ever take ourselves too seriously.

14. As you get to know your co-workers, identify who the real winners are, and gravitate toward them. Emulate their styles. Find out what sets the most successful people apart from the others, and use that knowledge to enhance your own selling efforts.

15. Avoid salespeople who are constantly negative or who are not doing well. These people have given up on themselves and have accepted themselves as losers. They can make you start to feel comfortable with the idea of losing, too. Losers always have excuses for losing, and they generally blame their customers, other salespeople, their company, their product, or their territory. There's always something, and you can be certain that it is never their fault!

16. The ability to react positively when a negative situation occurs is one of the most important skills you need to develop if you are to consistently do your best and become a winner. There is almost no situation in life, no matter how negative, from which you cannot extract something positive. Always doing your best despite adversity should become a habit for you, a way of life, a winning way of life!

17. It is very difficult to always do your best on a day-to-day basis for one simple reason: Consistency is not very exciting. That's why it really takes a tremendous amount of dedication and character to do your best, and then keep

doing it. Quitters quit. Winners—real winners—do not.
18. To be successful, you must be consistent. Be where you are supposed to be, do what you are supposed to do, and be on time, all the time!
19. Lazy, irresponsible, and careless people fail. Hardworking, responsible people with plans and enthusiasm succeed. These are the winners!
20. If you want to beat your competition *50* percent of the time, you must show up on time and go to work. The literal definition of the word "power" is the ability to take action.
21. If you want to beat your competition *75* percent of the time, you must show up on time, have a plan of action ready to go, and then go to work!
22. If you want to beat your competition *100* percent of the time, you must work harder, start earlier, stay later, plan more thoroughly, stick with it longer, show more intensity, and make more of a commitment to winning than your competition is willing to make.
23. Consider your competition, learn their attitudes about business, and exert yourself more than they are willing to exert themselves. There is magic in bold action. Take chances. Exert yourself . . . and expect miracles.

Dealing with Objections

To many salespeople, objections are like rabbits to a bird dog. Objections lead them down the wrong trail and cause them to become ineffective. I can't possibly count the number of sessions I've had with salespeople who were convinced they lost sales because they didn't know how to deal with an objection. Well, salespeople, the truth is that you virtually *never* lose a sale because of an objection. You lose a sale because you get sidetracked trying to deal with an objection that has little or nothing to do with the sale. I believe that many salespeople could double the number of sales they make if they would learn and apply the following principles on dealing with objections:

1. Good salespeople are able to answer almost any objection presented to them. There are only a limited number of actual objections, and the well-prepared salesperson has thought through the best way to deal with each one before it comes up.

2. Every objection presented by a customer *can* and *should* be transformed by the salesperson into a reason to buy. Trust me, if you think this issue through ahead of time, you will be able to do this. Let me repeat: There are only so many actual objections, and you should make plans on how to handle them before any objection comes up.

3. Good salespeople study the objections they might encounter in the field and prepare the best possible responses to those objections before they hear them from their customers. A good salesperson should never have to say, "Oops!"

4. Good salespeople usually hear very few objections. They have developed their presentations so effectively that they are able to prevent most objections. When I'm training salespeople and demonstrate an effective presentation, I often hear someone say,"I could have sold that one! Your customer didn't have any objections!" They seldom understand why.

5. Answering a customer's objections will never sell a product or service on its own. The only way any sale is truly made is by building value. If the customer is not sold on value, he will have an endless stream of objections.

6. When the perceived value of your product or service exceeds the price you are asking for it in your customer's eyes, that customer buys. At that point, the customer doesn't want to hear his own objections. If the perceived value does not exceed your asking price, the customer will inevitably state objections. Those objections have little if anything to do with his real reasons for deciding not to buy.

7. When objections arise, the amount of value you must build to overcome those objections will vary from customer to customer. For example, when customers worry about the disapproval of a spouse, you have to make them want your product or service so badly that they are willing to risk catching hell. Of course, some spouses are meaner than others, and only your customer can know just how much hell he or she is likely to catch! Your task then is to keep adding value until the customer decides that the risks of buying are less important than all the rewards of buying that you have identified.

8. Objections are reflections of your customers' fears. And, like most fears, these objections almost never actually materialize as problems for the customer.

9. Don't bother arguing with your customer. You can't win. If, on the other hand, you acknowledge your customer's objections and then build value to offset them, you can't lose.

10. It is usually a very good sign if you receive objections from a customer before you begin making your presentation. That customer knows that he or she can be sold. These early objections are almost always just a weak effort to build a barrier between the customer and the buying decision.

11. When handling objections, always let the customer talk first. There's an old saying from where I grew up that goes, "The first liar doesn't have a chance." When you answer objections that the customer hasn't expressed, it becomes much easier for him or her to rebut whatever you say, and frustrate your efforts to sell.

12. As I've stated, the best way to overcome any objection is to *build value.* If you build enough value into your product or service, the customer will find a way to overcome or simply disregard his or her objections, and move ahead to the purchase.

13. The more your customers consider the value and the benefits of your products or services, the less important their objections become. Acknowledge the objection, or ignore it and continue to build value.

Callbacks and Contingency Sales . . . or How to Lose an Order and a Career

This lesson is dedicated to those Elite Salespeople who make their sales with only one call on the customer. I call them "one-call closers." These wonderfully creative salespeople are my heroes. I became a one-call closer myself in 1977 after reading the book *How I Raised Myself from Failure to Success in Selling,* by Frank Bettger. This book is the fourth best book ever written on sales . . . after my three books! It changed my life, as I hope my books will change your life.

I read an article in the newspaper that reminded me of some of my own salespeople who call themselves one-call closers but who nevertheless make callbacks. It was about a man in Georgia who died following a rattlesnake bite. He had brought the snake to church, because the Bible says believers "shall take up serpents." The sheriff's department was not called, and later the death was ruled accidental.

What a shame! A church, which should be a safe haven from physical harm, became a deathtrap for this man. But think this story through with me, and see the similarities between this incident and making a callback or a contingency sale.

First, it was self-induced. The man did not *have* to pick up the snake. By the same token, you do not *have* to make a callback. Your program makes it possible to sell with one call, 100 percent of the time, doesn't it? If your program does not allow you to sell on one call, then you won't be a one-call closer. If it does, stick to it. Have enough courage to demand a yes or no answer from your prospects. Be man or woman enough to take that yes or no.

Second, the man's death was stupid and illogical. He knew that the snake he was handling was poisonous and might bite. Even the snake tried to warn him of the danger by rattling his tail. I believe there is something innate inside all of us that tells us to avoid harmful things, like stepping on hot coals with our bare feet or picking up poisonous snakes.

If you are a one-call closer, it is simply stupid to make callbacks. You *have* been told they don't work, haven't you? The good salespeople in your organization don't make them, do they? You've been warned that they will kill your career, haven't you? If you haven't been warned in the past, then I am warning you now! Don't make callbacks!

Third, what could have and should have been a great religious experience for the Georgia man became a tragedy. He turned a blessing into a curse! The same can be said of a sales call. Whether you sell or not, you will come out a winner if you stay on your program. You can leave with pride whether or not the sale is closed if you called the shots. However, you become a beggar and a loser if you call yourself a one call-closer but still make callbacks.

Finally, snake handling doesn't pay off. Even if that snake didn't kill him, the next snake or next probably would have. If you handle enough snakes, you will eventually be bitten.

If you make callbacks, they will eventually kill you too! The terrible thing about callbacks is that they will weaken you so much that you will never be a successful one-call closer. Callbacks don't just rob you of your time and opportunity. They also rob you of your self-respect.

Principles

1. Your product or service can always be sold on a one-call basis—no exceptions.

2. You should not take an order that you cannot sell on one call—no exceptions.

3. The more contingency orders you sell, and the more callbacks you make, the worse your delivery and sales volume will be . . . and the more frustrated you will become.

4. If a customer doesn't buy now, he or she will usually never buy. You should accept that fact, and make sure the customers know it, too. They will not get "hotter" after you leave. They will inevitably get colder. Spend all your precious time and effort on that high-percentage *first* call!

PHONY REASONS TO MAKE CALLBACKS . . . AND THE REASONS WHY YOU SHOULDN'T

"The customer couldn't decide between two options."

Good, strong salespeople don't offer options. Remember that *you* are the expert, and your customers should take *your* advice, especially if they are indecisive.

Customers always cool down after a sales presentation. I would hate to think that a customer might get more excited about my product after I leave than he was while I was with him!

Your customer's family and friends who did not see your sales presentation will inevitably talk him out of making the purchase.

Customers are able to think of a thousand reasons why they need to postpone the sale if they set their mind to do so.

If you agree to come back for their first excuse, they know you will probably come back for the next excuse, also.

There is simply no satisfying some customers. You might as well find out if your customer is one of these as soon as possible if you have anything else worthwhile going on that could make better use of your time. Have these customers fish or cut bait.

It is always worth whatever extra work is necessary to get a yes or no *now!*

If you do *not* sell him on the first call, you are cheating him out of ever having your product, and cheating yourself out of the sale.

"I need to get approval from somebody else."

You should never hear this excuse, because you should have qualified *before* you started your presentation that your customer was the decision maker. If you do hear this statement, simply walk away from this sale. Use the experience as a lesson that will remind you to properly qualify your next customer.

What credentials on your product or service does this person with approval authorization have? *You* are the expert. The customer should listen to you, and take your advice.

Tell your customer that the silent partner whom he failed to mention before you started your presentation must now remain silent.

Tell the customer that if it is necessary for him or her to ask for a spouse's permission to buy, you had better ask your spouse's permission to sell. (Use this one advisedly!)

The best way to close in a situation like this is simply to tell the customer the truth. You might say something like, "Mr. Customer, your (party in question) might tell you *no,* and if you don't buy now, you will *never* have my product or service. Is that what you want? Someone to tell you *no?* If so, I will tell you no, and we can part friends."

"I might want more of your product or service than you're offering now" (the "deluxe model, " etc.).

Sell the customer what you are selling *now.* Say, "This is the one I have a special on today."

Say, "We can upgrade the order later if you take advantage of the special offer I'm making today."

"What I want is something that you are not sure your company provides."

As a salesperson, you should know exactly what your company provides, and all the terms and conditions of the sale. Make sure the customer understands not only what you have, but what he or she really wants.

"I'm undecided on what method I'm going to use to pay off the contract."

Ask the customer to give you a deposit now and sign a five-week contract. Then say, "Now you have five weeks to come up with alternative financing!"

Say, "You must come up with the deposit now to take advantage of my special offer."

The customer asks for the sale to be made contingent on a future event, such as the approval of a bank loan, etc.

This one is simple: *Never* make a contingency sale! Next to a callback, it is the most damaging thing that salespeople can do to themselves.

When a customer requests a contingency, you don't really have a sale . . . you have only the *promise* of a sale. And as you well know, you can't live on promises.

Accept the fact that most contingency sales never materialize. Even if the required "contingency" comes to pass, it gives the customer time to come up with other excuses why he or she shouldn't go through with the purchase. These situations usually end up wasting a lot of your time, and they are demoralizing.

"I want you to take a postdated check."

Professional salespeople don't take postdated checks.

Say, "Please don't embarrass yourself and me by having me turn in that postdated check. My company would laugh at me."

Or say, "No, I have all of those I can use in my desk drawer. I need something I can turn into cash right now."

Your customer asks you to alter your company's contract guarantees, the terms and conditions of the sale, etc.

If your customer asks you to do anything that you would have to keep secret from your company, walk away. Follow this simple rule. Ask yourself, "If I make this sale, will I win? Will my customer win? Will my company win?" If the answer to any of these questions is no, don't make the sale.

You know that your customer does not understand all the conditions of the sale, or his or her obligations resulting from the sale.

Your goal should *not* be 100 percent delivery. You should never be satisfied with anything less than 100 percent customer *satisfaction*. This may require spending a little extra time confirming that the customer is clear about every aspect of the transaction, including contract terms, delivery and payment schedules, etc.

Principles

1. The contract and paperwork for every sale should be completed and correct before you leave the customer's place of business. The customer should understand and agree to all the terms and conditions of the sale.

2. About 75 percent of contingency orders are never delivered. Think about the long-term implications of a selling situation before you consider entering into a contingency arrangement. Your record and reputation as a professional salesperson will ultimately be much more important to you than some small financial remuneration you might receive now.

3. About 75 percent of the problem orders and cancellations that sales-based companies face are caused by contingencies, incompetence, or deception on the part of salespeople who are too eager to obtain a signature and not eager enough to satisfy their customers.

KEEP IN MIND

If you call yourself a one-call closer, remember this: Anytime you find yourself tempted to say, "I'll come back another time," "Give me a call," "I'll call you," or "I'll check in with you later," etc., do the following.

1. Realize that you are in great danger of ruining your career. Callbacks *will* ruin your career!

2. Put all your paperwork and other materials into your briefcase and prepare to leave. Do this slowly and deliberately.

3. Shake hands with your customer and thank him for his time. Be cheerful and pleasant, but firm.

4. Say, "Let's not kid ourselves. If I leave here without an order, you're going to cool down and you'll never buy my product or service. People you know who haven't seen my presentation will be negative about this, and talk you out of buying.

"If you want my product or service, buy it now. If you can't buy it now, I'm just not interested in selling it to you. I must find a customer who will buy now!"

5. At this point, walk away and leave clean . . . with or without the order. And whatever you do, don't go back. Don't call back, don't crawl back, and don't even think back about that call. Go out and find fresh meat every day.

6. Follow these guidelines 100 percent of the time. Work hard, and you will have spectacular success.

Rarely does a single characteristic or practice have as much impact on a career as becoming a one-call closer and sticking with it. Try it, make it work for you, and watch your commissions soar!

GENIUS

"Doing easily what others find difficult is talent; doing what is impossible for talent is genius." (Henri F. Amiel, *Amiel's Journal,* December 17, 1856)

I tell you, it is possible to do what many salespeople say is not possible! For many years I have sold a big-ticket item on a one-call basis. I didn't make an appointment with my prospects, and did not work leads. I was successful at working this plan 100 percent of the time without ever making a single callback. I would receive a minimum deposit of 20 percent from my customers. I had them make their check out to me, and I went to the bank and cashed it immediately. I have taught hundreds of dealers and managers how to do the same thing. Keep in mind that in the business I'm in, most sales are not finally closed until the *twelfth* call. Well, we do it in one call.

I consider true one-call closers the real geniuses of sales. They truly do what others believe is impossible. To these sales experts, I say, "I respect you, admire you, and love you. Good luck and good selling!"

Closing the Sale

I always spend a lot of time teaching my dealers how to close the sale. The reason for this is simple. If they don't close a sale, they don't make any money. Over the years I've developed eighty-eight distinctive closes that I use to fit virtually any situation. I believe that, given the opportunity, I could close anyone. As I said earlier, I've made a career out of selling big-ticket items on a one-call basis without appointments, and I've never made a callback. I collected 20 percent of the purchase price at the time of sale. With conditions like those, you *have* to be a strong closer! At one point in my career, I sold fifty-eight out of sixty presentations. That, my friend, is closing the sale on a grand scale! The message here is simple: If you are ever going to be successful in sales, you *must master* the art of closing.

Principles

1. What is a close? A close is anything that we say or do to cause the customer to buy now!

2. Closing a sale is easy when a customer wants the product or service you are offering. The close is difficult or impossible if you have not first built enough *value* for the customer.

3. When customers want your product or service badly enough, they will usually *tell* you how they can be sold. Listen to your customers carefully, and respond appropriately to what they say.

4. A close will be difficult to complete successfully if your customer is confused in any way. Make sure all of your presentation is clear and concise. Be sure your customers know all the terms and conditions of the sale, and all the costs they will be expected to pay.

5. Maintain control of the close. Stick to your agenda, and don't allow yourself to be sidetracked by your customer's agenda. Act as though you *should* be in control and *expect* to be in control.

6. Keep your prime objective in mind at all times. The reason for making any special offer is to get a signed order from your customer *now*. If your customer won't buy now, make sure he knows that he won't get the special offer.

7. Remember, however, that customers won't believe that your special offer is sincere if they don't see how *you* will also benefit from the transaction. The customer knows that you aren't Santa Claus. As you build value for your customer, you must simultaneously build value for *yourself* to justify any special offer you make.

8. Closing is work . . . work that requires real determination. Strong and decisive salespeople close their sales. Weak and indecisive salespeople are closed out of sales. Remember this simple formula: For every presentation you make, you will either *close* your customer or he will *close you out*.

9. You already know that the three most important ingredients in any sale are *value, urgency,* and *clarity.* The three most important ingredients in any close are *preparation, self-confidence,* and *determination.*

10. No close can ever be effective if the customer does not want the product or service you are offering. To help you convince your customer that he or she really wants what you are selling, be sure to build value like a millionaire, but lower price like a miser.

11. What is value? The meaning of the term "value" varies

from customer to customer. You must understand how to build value in any circumstance you may encounter. Understanding what is of value to your customer, and incorporating that value into your product of service, is the essence of selling and closing the sale.

12. An expression I often use with my salespeople is "Construction will not lead to seduction!" This simply means that spending lots of time describing the features of your product or service will seldom lead you to an effective close. *Value* is the only reason why customers buy.

13. Since every close works more effectively when the customer really wants the product or service being offered, you can take advantage of one common human characteristic that salespeople rarely talk about . . . greed. You'll be amazed to find how appealing to your customer's greed to get your product at a special price can break down resistance and cause your close to work like magic.

14. The most common type of close used by salespeople is the price discount. This is also the most misunderstood close, because too many salespeople don't realize that a lowered price will never motivate customers to buy something they don't really want. All a lowered price can do is motivate people to buy something they truly want *now* rather than postponing their purchase to a later time.

15. If your customers want your product or service badly enough, they will always find a way to pay for it. You will never meet a customer who is too broke to buy something he wants badly enough.

16. The best closing techniques in our business are really extensions of the same value builders that we've used earlier in our presentation. For example, you might have explained to your customer that the money saved through purchasing your product will pay the rent for the business. You can then build on this point of value and use it as one more reason for the customer to buy when you make your closing presentation.

17. Words of assurance from you, the expert, as well as support from the customer's friends and family—people whom the customer trusts—are probably among the most effective closing techniques of all.

18. Your customer's family, friends, and customers can be a big help to you when you sell your product or service. If they are approached properly, they will usually agree that the purchase is a wise one. After all, they can afford to be big spenders, because the sale you make to your customer won't cost them a dime!

19. Taking something in trade from your customer can be another effective closing technique. Here, the mutual benefits for you and your customer are clear. Your customer not only wants your product or service but wants to "sell" you his as well. If you deduct his retail price from your cost, your customer is getting a 50 percent discount, because that is what he paid for the product.

20. You will find that your best customers tend to be those who have already purchased something from you in the past. You already know they must like what you are offering. If they didn't, they wouldn't have bought from you in the first place. These customers will appreciate any special offer you make, and can probably afford to buy more.

21. Conversely, your worst customers will tend to be those who have never purchased from you in the past. These new prospects must first be sold on the value of what you are offering. Then, they have to be educated about your product or service. Finally, they have to be closed on a commitment to buy. Of course, your customers might think they are broke, unable to afford anything you have to offer. They are wrong, of course, but for these customers, you must build tremendous value to overcome their false preconceptions.

22. Whenever your prospects offer you some small favor such as a cup of coffee or tea, accept it gratefully. The best way to ingratiate yourself with a customer is to let him or her do *you* a favor . . . especially during the closing phase of your presentation.

23. Every customer wants to feel special, and every customer naturally wants to believe that he or she is getting a special deal. It doesn't cost you a penny to make your customer feel special with compliments or special attention.

24. Never be more anxious to sell than the customer is to buy. Take time during your close, and allow your customer to warm up to the idea of buying *now*.

25. The only time to close any sale is when the customer knows everything he or she needs to know in order to make an intelligent buying decision, and is ready to say yes right now.

26. Explain to your customer why buying your product or service *now* is the right thing to do. At the same time, make it clear why not buying now would be both an illogical and foolish choice.

27. Customers almost always need a logical reason to buy *now*, on your terms, rather than later, on their terms. It is your responsibility as a salesperson to make buying *now* the sensible thing for your customer to do.

28. Getting that yes response *now* should always be your reasonable expectation. Handling yourself as if you expect the customer to buy now is a powerful closing technique that sets the stage for a successful sale.

29. You will find that if you try to close a sale early just because the customer starts to show some initial buying signs, it will usually wind up like other things you do prematurely. You and your customer will both be frustrated and disappointed.

30. Always remember that closing the sale is payday for most salespeople. The math is simple: The more successful closes you make, the more you earn. It is therefore *in your best interest* to master the art of closing. Strong closers are always the highest-paid salespeople!

31. Don't bother looking for new ways to close. Look for new ways to build value! It is easy to close an eager buyer who has recognized the special value that only your product or service will provide.

32. Remember that despite any protests your customers

may raise, they *want* to be sold. If they didn't want to be sold, they would never have agreed to talk with you in the first place. When a customer gives you his or her time and agrees to look at your product, you are being invited to make the sale. But it's up to you to figure out how to do it properly by building value for that particular customer!

33. Don't allow that stale old excuse, "I don't have the money," to stand in your way. Actually, when customers tell you this, you should read it as a very positive buying signal. Why? It means that they have considered buying your product or service and are now trying to figure out how they can pay for it. Think about it for a moment. When a customer makes an absolute decision against buying, he or she usually communicates the "no" message as quickly as possible. Why waste more time if the decision has been made? And why would a customer worry about money if he or she weren't already thinking seriously about making a purchase?

34. Objections that are stated "up front" by your customers are also good buying signs. Such objections often arise because customers intuitively sense that they are likely to buy, and feel they must protect themselves from making a financial commitment.

35. The most difficult customers to sell are those who tell you they are anxious to look at your proposal and hear your presentation. These people are confident of their ability to turn you down, and therefore have no reservations about listening to whatever you have to say. These are the customers who will usually have no trouble telling you no when you attempt to close the sale.

36. Your close should always come as the logical conclusion to your well-thought-out, carefully planned, and professionally delivered presentation. It is the closing chapter of your well-crafted story.

37. The most effective closing tool you have available to you is your expectation that the customer will say yes. I

have repeated this point because I want you to understand how important it is. Some salespeople are surprised or nervous when the customer says yes quickly. Don't be! It's what you want to hear!

38. If you have done your job properly, you will get either a yes or no at the end of your presentation. If you do your job convincingly, you will inevitably hear yes more often than no.

39. If you are a good auto mechanic, you can repair most types of cars. If you are a good doctor, you are able to cure many different illnesses. If you are a good salesperson, you are able to close successfully most of the time, no matter what the customer may raise as a concern or objection.

40. Remember that your time is a valuable commodity. The more time you spend with a customer, the less you are able to earn from the total amount of time you have available to you. In fact, salespeople are among the only professionals who earn *less* the longer they work with a particular customer!

41. You should always expect to be paid at the end of every presentation you make. The only way you can accomplish this is to close at the end of every presentation.

42. "When your customer tells you 'I'll think it over and let you know' . . . you know." (Olin Miller) By the way, if you ever hear this line, you should let your customer *know* you know, and make *sure* he knows.

The Price of Your Product or Service

Certainly, the most overrated factor in the minds of new salespeople is the price of the product or service they sell. Most salespeople are overly concerned about the price of their product or service. Many think that if they could just lower their price below that of the competition, the customer would naturally and inevitably buy from them. In fact, this is generally not true.

Price is only one factor in the total selling process, and it is certainly not the most important one. In fact, on a scale of one to ten in relative importance, price would rank near the bottom. *Value* is at the top of that scale. That's why you need to master the art of building value, and develop the self-discipline to resist your impulse to lower your price until it is truly to your advantage to do so.

A major difference between professional salespeople and order takers is that salespeople routinely and effectively negotiate the price of their product or service. Most people think that negotiating the price means lowering the price, but this is not always the case. True salespeople develop a sense of *value* for their products or services. They know that the price of the product or service they represent is based strictly on how much value they can create in the mind of their customer.

131

I once took four of my dealers and managers into the field to demonstrate this aspect of building value. With four witnesses at my side, I sold a sign that we regularly sold for $795 for $7,995. Weak salespeople reduce their price too soon and too much, and reducing your price too soon and too much only makes your weaker and weaker.

Principles

1. Whenever customers tell you that your price is too high or they don't have enough money, they are really telling you that you haven't yet built enough value for them to buy the product or service you are offering.

2. The average salespersons drops his or her price too soon, too often, and by too much. That kind of quick acquiescence shows weakness, and is the mark of a sales amateur.

3. Customers cannot know for certain whether or not they will buy until they have all the facts they need. First, they must carefully consider *all* the benefits of any product or service. The more your customers consider the value and benefits of your product or service, the more likely they will be to find a way to afford it. It's as if a chemical reaction takes place within your customers that causes them to buy, but *you* have to set the right temperature, make the time, and create the other environmental conditions that allow this reaction to take place!

4. When you're broke or desperate to make a sale, you'll find it difficult to tell yourself that money is not a problem. If you should unintentionally communicate your anxiety about finances to your potential customers, they are likely to become "infected" with your attitude. Chances are your customers will tell you that they don't have any money and can't buy your product now. Just remember that, as a salesperson, you are also an actor. Always place yourself in the role of the millionaire salesperson, and you will soon discover that everyone will be able to afford the products or services you are selling!

5. Don't discount or undervalue the product or service

you sell. In the hands of a truly professional salesperson, almost any product or service can make magic.

6. The value of your product or service is determined by three distinct factors. First is your customer's *general impression* of its value. This impression is generally limited and sometimes inaccurate. Your customer is usually not an expert on the value of your product or service, and sometimes makes mistakes. It is part of your job to correct any false impressions your customers may develop.

Second is the *confidence* and *trust* the customer has in the salesperson's assessment of his or her product or service. The more professional and knowledgeable you are, the more confidence your customers will have in you.

Third is the *price* you place on your product or service. You can often raise the value of your product or service by raising your price. Just be aware that each time you lower your price, you are also lowering the value of your product or service in the eyes of your customer.

7. Before you actually reduce your price, be sure to build more value in your customer's mind first to compensate for the lower value your price reduction will naturally create in the mind of your customer.

AFTER THE SALE

A common mistake made by many salespeople is thinking that after the sale is made, the job is over. Many bad things can happen after the sale is closed if you let your guard down and become careless. A customer might change his mind and put a "stop payment" on the check written for you. Another customer might not understand all the terms and conditions of the sale you made and come to believe that you've taken unfair advantage him or her. A sales professional will always act like a pro before, during, *and* after the sale. I have seen too many orders that were lost because careless salespeople did not maintain their professionalism after the customer agreed to buy.

Principles

1. When a customer says yes, shake his hand and congratulate him on his purchase. Don't ever take a sale for granted just because a customer says he will buy. That person can very easily change his mind if you don't continue building value as you complete the paperwork.

2. Be sure to fill out all of your paperwork carefully, completely, and confidently. Prepare it for your customer's signature. Uncertainty at this point has also led to many lost sales.

3. When you complete your paperwork, review it thoroughly before offering it to your customer. Then, ask your customer to review and sign the contract.

4. Be sure to thank everyone involved in the sale. Finally, make sure that the customer knows and understands all the issues related to billing and delivery of your product or service.

5. Every sale you make should be a sale in which you can take genuine pride. Remember, there must always be three winners in every sale. You must win. The company you represent must win. But the big winner must always be your customer!

The Double-Minded Man

Have you ever felt that you weren't getting anywhere in your career or in your life? Have you ever felt that no matter what you did or how much effort you put into something, it always turned out badly? Have you ever felt frustrated, discouraged, or disillusioned? Would you like to become more effective, and see your projects and priorities start to succeed? Well, read on as I describe what I think is one of the most important considerations in determining individual success and accomplishment.

In Jas. 1:8, the Bible says, "A double-minded man is unstable in all his ways." This passage is clear. It tells us that if you are "double-minded"—that is, if you are indecisive, unfocused, and noncommittal—your life will be unstable and shaky. I have worked with hundreds of salespeople over the years and have seen a full range of personalities. Some have been winners, and some have been losers. I've tried to analyze what characteristics separate the winners from the losers and have come to this one simple conclusion: "A double-minded man" is inherently unstable, especially in his professional life. One good indication of this is a person who is working at two or more jobs. If he would focus his energies on just one job, he would ultimately be more productive and reap greater rewards.

Of course, being double-minded and uncertain can make *any* situation unstable. Consider, for example, a wife who says to her husband, "I'm not sure whether I want to spend the rest of my life with you or with John." Anyone would have to consider that marriage unstable. Most people agree that athletes who are not single-minded and dedicated to their sport will never have much success. To be a winner at anything you must first *desire* the victory, and be willing to pay a higher price for it than anyone else. If you cannot decide whether you want to excel at football, ice skating, bowling, or golf, you probably won't excel at any one of them.

Now think about the situation facing a person who is unsure about his religion. He might say to himself, "I want to have the security of a believer, but Baptists don't dance, so that's out. I like a short worship service like the Catholics have, but if I become a Catholic, I can't have two wives, like the Mormons. I also like to have drink now and then. And I'm certainly not going to turn over 20 percent or so of what I earn to the church, so that means I can't become a Mormon. Maybe I'll become Jewish. But I don't want to be persecuted, so maybe I should be a . . ."

The point here is that if we do not make a meaningful commitment, nothing will turn out well. Given this fact, what can we do to become more "single-minded," especially in business, and strive for professional success more effectively? Well, consider the following ideas that can be helpful for salespeople and managers at all levels in an organization.

NEW SALESPEOPLE

1. If you want to succeed in sales, you should first put on a set of professional blinders. Why? To keep yourself from getting sidetracked! Work on your presentation until you can say it perfectly and convincingly. Master every aspect of your business right from the very start.

2. If you decide that something is not worth all your effort, then don't waste any more of your valuable time on

it. Being a great salesperson is a lot like being a fine athlete. You must be "single-minded" from the very beginning. Don't allow yourself to be sidetracked or discouraged by others. Once you set your goals, keep them in sight at all times. Don't waiver. You'll need to give 100 percent of your best effort if you are to succeed. Remember that no one ever succeeds by accident. You've never heard anyone say, "Oops!" when he achieves success. Whenever people succeed at anything, they do so only because they intended to do so and worked hard to do so.

EXPERIENCED SALESPEOPLE

1. You will not continue to succeed in this business if you approach it half-heartedly. When you're sure of what you are doing, selling becomes easy. If you are unsure, if you are not convinced about what you are doing, then you will have a very difficult time convincing others to buy from you.

2. I have often observed salespeople take on other responsibilities, such as part-time jobs, just when they start to succeed in their first job. This only dissipates their energies, and they don't do well at either job.

3. It is vitally important for you to *know* and *believe* that your company's program works. Focus all of your energy on what you do best. Make the most of the opportunity that you think has the most promise.

4. What could you accomplish if you prepared yourself for salesmanship in the same way professional boxers prepare themselves for a big fight? Some things they do often include:

Preparing for at least three months before the fight by controlling their weight and avoiding alcohol and tobacco.

Training—running, sparring, doing calisthenics, and hitting a punching bag for at least eight to ten hours each day.

Practicing and perfecting their boxing skills until every move they make becomes second nature to them.

Studying their opponents carefully until they know everything about their fighting style.

Making certain that their *equipment* is completely in order.

Many *abstain* from sex until they win the fight. (Now *that* would be a real incentive for salespeople to make the sale!)

5. Are you already on the way to becoming a champion salesperson? If your answer is no, then here's the simple reason why: You are not willing concentrate, work, and train the same way that champions do! In other words, you are a double-minded person.

MANAGERS

1. Are you really serious about building your sales organization? Do you want to make your group the most successful in your entire organization within the next few months or years? Well, put this plan of action into effect immediately, and see what happens.

2. Plan to meet with your sales staff six days a week, every week, and be on time every time. (Remember that being "on time" for a manager means being *early*. You're the one who unlocks the door and makes the first pot of coffee. *You* are the first one into the office in the morning.)

3. Invest however many hours may be necessary for you to train your people so they can succeed.

4. Run your business in the way a business should be run. Open the door, and go to work every day. Care about your salespeople. Study your trade, and put forward your maximum effort.

5. If you just took these simple steps, you would be set for life! Remember that halfway measures, on-again, off-again efforts, or energy that's expended in fits and starts will lead inevitably to frustration and instability. "Stick with your stuff," be single-minded in your effort, and everything will come your way.

Consider what some notable people have said on this topic.

"Opportunities are usually disguised as hard work, so most people don't recognize them." (Ann Landers)

"An optimist sees an opportunity in every calamity; a pessimist sees a calamity in every opportunity." (Sir Winston Churchill)

"Amateurs hope. Professionals work." (Garson Kanin)

"Perseverance: A lowly virtue whereby mediocrity achieves an inglorious success." (Ambrose Bierce)

"Pay as little attention to discouragement as possible. Plough ahead as a steamer does, rough or smooth . . . rain or shine." (Maltbie D. Babcock)

"There is no security on this earth . . . there is only opportunity." (Douglas MacArthur)

Family Involvement

One of the most important elements in the success or failure of salespeople is the cooperation and involvement of their family. If your spouse is unhappy with your sales career, you'll have little chance of succeeding. If your spouse does not respect the time and commitment you must invest to learn your craft properly, you will have little chance of success. I've seen good salespeople fail just because they were compelled by an uncooperative spouse to take their kids to school or pick them up. Driving your spouse to or from work or other infringements on your professional time will all but destroy your chances for success in sales. On the other hand, a spouse who cooperates, helps, and encourages his or her mate can be a salesperson's most valuable asset.

Principles
1. Poor work and money-management habits are the primary reasons why good salespeople fail, but the third key reason is a lack of cooperation from families.

2. Enlist the help of your family as you plan, study, prepare, and commit yourself to your career in sales. Get a commitment of cooperation and understanding from them.

3. Don't gripe at home. Never criticize your employer, your company's products, or your co-workers when you are with your family, no matter how frustrating a day

you've had at work. Never complain to your family about your income or the difficulties you're having getting started in sales. Your complaints will slowly turn your family against your company or product and make it doubly difficult for you to succeed.

4. Now I'd like to get a bit personal for a moment. Over the years, I've learned that some new salespeople are unable to handle the freedom that their new sales careers offer. All too often, they take advantage of their newfound freedom to cheat on their family. (Note that I used the word "family" here . . . not just spouse. That word choice is purposeful. Cheating does not just harm a "spouse" but an entire family unit, including yourself.) Exercise maturity and self-control! You owe it to yourself and those who truly care about you.

5. If you cannot obtain the support, approval, and cooperation of your spouse as you pursue your sales career, you may want to consider another line of work.

6. Your financial success probably won't seem very important if someday you look have to back and see that this same success led to a broken home.

7. Spouses, cooperate with and support your salesperson partner, and it will pay you big dividends. If you do not cooperate, you may be condemning both of you to a life of failure. There is nothing so demoralizing after a hard day's work than to be greeted at home by a demanding, cold-hearted spouse.

Evoking Trust

Much more important to a salesperson than a glib tongue or a good personality is the ability to evoke trust. I've found that many salespeople are just too clever for their own good. They have mastered the techniques for selling their product or service. They may know how to overcome objections and build value, but they still cannot close many sales, and they can't understand why they have a problem. The reason is simply that the customers *don't trust them.* These salespeople become very frustrated when they see a less skillful salesperson call on the same customer and pick up the sale easily . . . only because the customer trusts him. Trust, like all other characteristics that successful sales professionals need, can be developed. Adhere to the following principles, and see your sales career skyrocket.

Principles

1. If you are completely trustworthy yourself, you will be trusted by your customers.

2. You will be trusted if you expect to be trusted, but you will be trusted even more if you *deserve* and expect to be trusted.

3. The single most important prerequisite for establishing your credibility is your own self-confidence. Self-confidence is an outgrowth of your personal integrity.

4. Whenever you demonstrate knowledge about your product or service, your company, and your profession, you enhance your personal and professional credibility.

5. When you behave professionally at all times with the customer, you enhance your credibility.

6. Your professional appearance also enhances your credibility with your customers.

7. People naturally tend to trust those who project an air of prosperity and professionalism. On the other hand, they tend to distrust shabby-looking people or those who seem unsure of themselves.

8. As a salesperson, *you are* the company from your customers' point of view. If your customers trust you, they will probably also trust the company you represent.

9. You can help enhance the professionalism of your company in many simple ways. For example, you can casually show photographs of your company's plant, offices, or products to your prospect during your presentation. This will help your customer visualize and more fully appreciate the organization you represent.

10. Everyone wants to do business with an expert who will help them overcome their lack of knowledge in certain areas. Quite often, you'll find that your customers are not sure that buying your product or service is the right thing to do. Therefore, the most effective thing you can do is to assure them that you are the expert and you know what is best for the customer. Do all the work you need to make sure that you are, in fact, the expert you want and need to be!

11. As I said, I believe that people are only able to evoke trust effectively when they themselves are trustworthy. The Bible says that if you want to make friends, you should be friendly. Well, doesn't that apply to trust in the same way? If you want to be completely trusted, you should be completely honest. Then, and only then, can you reasonably expect to be trusted.

12. As a salesperson, your primary professional objective should always be to help your customers. If you focus more of your attention on helping your customers than on making your commission, you will be trusted and respected.

13. Expect to be trusted. Never do or say anything in an effort to prove that you are honest. Anyone who does this simply raises doubts about credibility that needn't have arisen in the first place. Assume that what you say can and will be believed by your customers without the need for any external "proof."

14. If you attempt to manipulate your customers on small points, you will inevitably cause them to lose trust in you.

15. Always talk straight with your customers. Don't try using rusty old psychological tricks to get your customers to say or do things you want them to say or do.

16. Listen carefully to what your customers have to say. People tend to trust you when you really listen to them because they believe that you really care about their concerns and opinions. When you listen, you will impress them with your integrity. And there's one more important benefit . . . when you listen carefully, your customers will often tell you exactly how to sell them what you have to offer.

SOME THOUGHTS FOR SALES MANAGERS

1. You've probably all heard the old expression, "Criticize the fault, but not the person." Well, I've always believed that this idea is fundamentally unsound. The first step toward becoming responsible is for a person to be accountable for his or her own actions. In the same way, the first step in teaching others to become responsible is to teach them to be accountable for their own actions.

2. If you are serious about helping your salespeople

succeed, you must talk straight to them. Make sure you let them know about their bad habits and what the consequences of repeating those bad habits will be. Encourage them to discard their bad habits and develop good ones.

3. People tend to trust intelligent people. If you practice the following five rules, you will amaze people with your intelligence:

Rule 1. Make very direct, to-the-point statements. Never be ambiguous.

Rule 2. Ask direct and specific questions about subjects that really matter.

Rule 3. Do not answer, or assist in answering, your own questions.

Rule 4. Listen very carefully to the answers given to your questions.

Rule 5. Respond appropriately to statements your customers make and the answers they give to your questions.

I believe that by practicing these five rules, you will raise your IQ by fifteen points or more. The points will show up where it counts, not on some analytical charts, but in the minds of your customers and all those with whom you do business.

And remember, projecting intelligence evokes trust.

How to Control Your Customer and Your Situation

When I first became a direct salesman, I realized I had to make changes in many areas of my life. One of the biggest necessary changes centered on the issue of *control* . . . control not only of myself, but of the selling situations I encountered. For many years, when I had been an internal salesman, I thought that the best way to sell was to accommodate my customers in every way I could. I always placed the preferences and desires of these customers above my own needs and concerns. The approach I was taking was not unlike that of almost every other salesperson I knew. The idea, simply stated, went like this: If you accommodate the customers, if you give them what they want and make them feel important, they will be much more likely to buy from you. I had been taught the old saw that every salesperson has heard at one time or another: "The customer is always right." What a misguided joke that old idea is!

When you first hear this old cliché, it seems like a reasonable idea, right? Well, that's what I thought at one time. It took me a while to learn the truth, and the real truth is that people do *not* buy something because a salesperson made them feel good, or important, or smart. They do *not* buy because they like the salesperson or because they've been accommodated by him or her. They buy for one reason only: They *want* the product or service that's being offered. They buy because the real value of the product or service exceeds the cost in their minds. In order for you to build the value of your product or service to reach that point with your customer, you must *control* the selling situation. Once I realized this simple truth, I developed techniques to assure that I would maintain control of every selling situation.

Nothing is more frustrating for any salesperson than to lose a sale because the selling situation got away from him or her. No matter what the cause may be—questions from customers, unexpected and unwelcome jokes, phone calls, or any of a thousand other intrusions—the loss of control can mean a lost sale. Often, the people who cause the loss of control do so unintentionally, but you suddenly find yourself in a nearly impossible situation. The sale can't succeed unless you regain control.

Salespeople must communicate a lot of information within a limited time before their customers can make intelligent buying decisions. To do that successfully, they must maintain control of the selling process. So, how do you maintain control of a sale, or regain control if it should be taken away from you? How do you compel your customers and everyone else involved in your presentation to pay attention to you? Well, consider the following suggestions.

CONTROL BY ALWAYS BEING A PROFESSIONAL

I've often told my salespeople that they should work to make their sales presentations more interesting than *any* possible distraction, no matter how extreme. To make my point, I often tell this true story from my own days on the road.

Jimmy Thumper and I were working the territory in and around Compton, California. One day, we found ourselves in a rough neighborhood where we knew that fights frequently broke out. As we were making our sales presentation to a convivial store owner, one of those fights erupted out on the street directly in front of the establishment.

Now, this wasn't your average fight. One guy was behind the wheel of his car, racing back and forth. He was trying to run down another guy who was armed with a cinder block. The man with the masonry stood there in the street like a crazed matador. As the car came toward him, he jumped to one side and struck out with the cinder block at either the car or the driver. Finally, the driver stopped his car and jumped out. He emerged carrying a large wooden club and lunged toward his adversary. The other guy didn't miss the opportunity. He slammed the cinder block into the side of the guy's head. Amazingly, the wounded man managed to stay on his feet. He staggered back to his car, reached into the glove compartment, and pulled out a large pistol. He turned and tried to draw a bead on the guy who had just struck him.

I may have left Kentucky a long time ago, but there's still enough hillbilly left in me to love watching a good fight! This one was getting to be a real humdinger. Jimmy and I both wanted to stop and look out the window to see how this battle would turn out. But believe it or not, our customer had become so engrossed in our presentation that he wouldn't let us turn away from him. He was so busy visualizing his future success, counting up his imagined profits, and dreaming of things that would come to him that he wasn't the least bit interested in the fight . . . and he didn't want us to be distracted by it, either.

The customer said to us, "Hey, that kind of thing happens here every day. Let's get on with the presentation, okay?" Like the young girl who is told she's beautiful for the very first time, he wanted to hear more, more, more. Jimmy and I started deliberately to distract this guy. Jimmy looked out the window and said, "Now, there's something you don't see everyday . . . two nuns in a knife fight!"

"Happens all the time around here," said the customer. "Tell me some more about this special offer you've been talking about."

I said to him, "Darn, when the nuns get into a knife fight

everyday, you know this is a tough neighborhood."

I have also sold in nude bars where my presentation had to compete against naked dancing girls. So take my word for it . . . if you can make your presentation more exciting than a fist fight, two nuns in a knife fight, or a naked dancing girl, you can be sure you'll always have an audience.

If you are a true professional, you'll maintain control of every selling situation you encounter! When you master your presentation so you can say it perfectly and convincingly, you'll always be able to find an audience. Everyone enjoys watching a professional at work. It stands to reason, then, that if you work to make yourself a true sales professional, people will always enjoy watching you do your job. Every element of your presentation, from your introduction through the close, should be *perfect*. Every move, every gesture you make, should be choreographed to create the greatest possible impact on your prospects. If you take the time to perfect your presentation, you'll have little difficulty maintaining control of every selling situation.

CONTROL THROUGH DRESS

My heart truly aches when I see how some people come into a new sales job, hoping for success. These people completely stack the deck against themselves, but still they hope against hope to make it in the competitive world of sales. Some of these people dress the way I once did when I worked in the field, cutting tobacco in Kentucky. Still others dress as if they were hoping to "hang out" backstage with rock bands.

These days, it isn't considered polite or tactful to criticize people for the way they dress. That would be unkind, you see, and unkindness is never acceptable. Besides, if you did say something, many of today's young people would snap back at you, saying something like, "Nobody tells me how to dress!"

How *dumb* people can sometimes be! If I'd never been trout fishing in my life, I would certainly hope that before I went, someone would advise me that it'd be a good idea to wear hip boots and a hat with a sun visor! Whenever I'm unsure about matters of dress, I always seek out the advice of someone who knows what is *appropriate* to help me achieve the best possible results.

Most people would never insist on wearing cowboy boots if they knew that they were going mountain climbing. The same basic principle applies when you are going out to sell. Get smart! Don't let your clothing become a handicap to your professional development. Dress for success, and dress for control. Minorities have every right, of course, to dress according to the traditions of their ethnic heritage, but experience tells me that this would probably cost them a lot of money. Whenever you make an unusual dress decision in sales, be sure you are prepared to pay the price— because your customer always has the right *not* to buy from you.

Everyone wants to do business with a celebrity. Simple logic should tell you that the more important you look, the more seriously people will take you and what you have to say. That same logic should also tell you that the way to dress for success is to *dress as though you are successful . . .* whether you already are or not!

Much has been said and written about how salespeople should dress. I've found, however, that most of what I've read on this subject doesn't stand up under "real world" field testing. In fact, some of what I've read and believed initially on this subject was both harmful and wrong.

For example, I was told not to wear expensive jewelry . . . but then I found that people tend to notice and talk to people more readily if they have expensive jewelry. I was told that if I dressed conservatively, people would take me more seriously. Well, I found that just the opposite was true. The most important factor in one's professional dress is *the initial impression you make.* If your first impression convinces the customer that you are a successful sales professional, then you are already well on your way to making the sale. How you dress won't sell your product or service, but it will make it easier for you to get the opportunity to demonstrate and discuss your product or service.

Principles

1. Like books, salespeople are often judged by their "covers." Generally, we have a very short time in which to make a good first impression. As I've stated earlier, people tend to treat important-looking people who dress appropriately, and with an air of success, with more respect. Customers are much more likely to stop what they're doing and listen to a person who looks important than they are for someone who does not.

2. As a professional salesperson, you should always dress well. Look and act like an important person who's able to make a real difference for the people you meet. Remember that everyone just naturally wants to do business with a winner. Make sure that you always look like one whenever you deal with prospective customers.

3. If you can't dress like a millionaire, drive a fancy car, or live a lifestyle like a person with lots of money, then *act . . .* just pretend you can, and do it with pride and style! Before you know it, you'll find yourself achieving the measure of success you've been pretending to have all along.

4. No matter how poor your wardrobe is or how low on funds you might be, there's always something you can do to improve your appearance. When you do what you can, other opportunities for making improvements soon start presenting themselves. You'll find yourself earning more money in a short while, and then you can improve your wardrobe any way you may want!

5. Ladies, if you dress like a hooker, then don't be surprised if you find yourself dealing with customers who want you, but not your product or service.

CONTROL THROUGH YOUR VOICE

The human voice is a powerful tool. It can evoke strong

emotions and sway firmly held convictions. Elections have been won and movements have been started by parties or programs that had the most powerful spokesperson. Voice control is, in fact, one of the most effective control techniques available to us. How you say something is often more important than what you actually say.

For example, you may at times find yourself with a customer who interrupts you, or who talks too much. Whenever this happens to me, I look the customer straight in the eye and say his name *emphatically*—just his name and nothing more. I then remain silent. This inevitably stops the customer, who pauses and listens. I then say, crisply and clearly, "Jim, what you are saying is very important to me, and I don't want to miss anything. Why don't you hold that thought until I'm through, okay?"

As that example demonstrates, silence can also be a powerful tool. It is written in the Bible that "even a fool, when he holdeth his peace, is counted wise" (Prov. 17:28). When you speak your words carefully and control your silences, people will always pay attention to you and consider carefully what you have to say.

CONTROL THROUGH USE OF THE CUSTOMER'S NAME

Whenever you say your customer's name sharply, he or she will listen to you. Regardless of your surroundings, whatever din and confusion may surround you, you can be certain that your prospect will hear his own name when you speak it in his presence. This may seem like a simple or obvious statement, but it is a fact that many salespeople overlook. Use it to your advantage, and you will profit by it.

CONTROL THROUGH YOUR GESTURES

Body language can also be an effective means of communicating with others. When I used to start my sales presentation,

I would lift my hands high into the air to emphasize the impressive dimensions of the signs I wanted to sell. I would then hold my hands in this position until everyone in the room was looking at me and listening to my message. If I happened to lose control of the presentation at any time, I'd repeat the gesture. Then, when I had people looking at me once again, I'd state very emphatically, "Now, this is very important to me, so pay attention. I don't want you to miss anything, okay?"

You can control the attention of large groups of people at one time if you put on a show that's worth watching. Your actions, like your words, should always be very concise and calculated to create the optimal effect. When you stand in a crowded room with your hand high, motionless and silent, you can't help but look like a person who has something very important to say. People *will* pay attention. They will listen to you.

Another technique you may want to consider has been very successful for me over the years. To gain control of a selling situation, I extend my hand as if I want to shake hands with my prospect. When that person takes my hand, I put my other hand on top of his or hers. At that point, I have that person's undivided attention. In a calm and cheerful voice, I then say something like, "Jim, this is very important to me. Do you want to see the rest of this presentation?" If he says yes, then I know I have the right to expect courtesy and attention from that point on. If he say no, he has the right to expect me to leave. Either way, I'm in control.

When you sell, always stand erect. Don't display any nervousness . . . and smile! Let your gestures demonstrate your pride and confidence in yourself and the products or services you are selling. Every gesture and movement you make in your sales presentation should be carefully and thoroughly rehearsed until you have mastered them, and can be certain of the positive impact they will have on your customers.

CONTROL THROUGH THE USE OF PROPS

Your product sample, if you have one, is without doubt

the best prop you have. But it isn't the only one available to you. What else do you have?

Well, consider: Your brochure book, briefcase, eyeglasses, magic markers, pictures of your product or service . . . any or all of these things can be used to help you make effective sales presentations. If you decide to work these items into your sale, practice with them until you've thoroughly mastered their use and can apply it smoothly and flawlessly. Your proposal, sketchpad, graphs, charts . . . these can all be used to help you gain and keep control. Used improperly, they can and will work against you, destroying your best efforts. It all depends on how you use them!

I find that big steel rulers can be effective tools for attracting and holding the attention of those I'm trying to sell. I just pull one out and start touching the ceiling with it. Soon, everyone in the place is wondering who the strange man with the ruler is, and why he's poking at the ceiling! They stop whatever they are doing, look at me, and listen to what I have to say. Once I sense that I have their attention, I hold on to it by saying something like, "What I'm saying is very important to me, and I think it will be important to you. Please pay attention. I don't want there to be any misunderstandings, okay?"

CONTROL THROUGH ENTERTAINMENT

I've always believed that I could compete with any distraction during my sales presentations. Every salesperson should develop this attitude. Commit yourself to putting on such informative and entertaining presentations that your customers will listen and pay attention to everything you have to say. If you are truly entertaining, your customers will hang on every word of your presentation.

CONTROL THROUGH A THIRD PARTY

Many salespeople consider third-party involvement in a sales presentation to be detrimental, or at least unproductive. I've always believed that additional people can be helpful allies when I'm trying to make a sale . . . if they are handled properly.

Often, when a family member or some other person is present, I'll find a way to use that person to help me tell my story to my customer. I've never, for example, dismissed the intrusive comments of a person who's had too much to drink. First, I'll tell a drunk to shut up. Then, when he looks at me, I tell him that I need his advice. Having done that, I am usually able to sell the customer *through* this person. The drunk becomes my advocate, and my selling job becomes easier!

One example of this sort of thing happened to me while I was making a sales call at Ken's bar in Columbus, Ohio. Shortly after I began my presentation to Ken, the owner, I found myself being heckled by a bearded drunk who wanted Ken to pour him another shot . . . or two. "Hey, what's your name?" I asked my tormentor.

"I'm Fred," he told me.

"Well, Fred," I responded, "do me a favor, and shut up!"

The bearded man rose angrily as if he wanted to throw a punch in my direction. I calmed him quickly when I said, "I need you to be quiet because I need your advice on something." He became mellow. I went on. "If you owned this bar, wouldn't you want this big sign out there, telling everybody that this is the place to be in this town?"

"Yeah, sure!" said Fred.

"Great! Then help me out by keeping those guys over there quiet, so can sell Ken a sign!"

From that point on, Fred was my ally, and he helped me make the sale. The point is simple. Get everyone on your side, and it becomes easy to sell because everybody around you wants you to do it.

CONTROL THROUGH SELF-CONTROL

A simple truth that few people understand is that the real

secret of controlling others is to control *yourself.* In fact, people who exercise self-control usually have no problem controlling others. The salesperson who plans his words and executes his actions with precision will be successful. The salesperson who is careless about himself *will* not and *should* not control others.

I used to adhere to a little axiom that summed up my attitude on the issue of control. More than once I've said to a potential customer, "Look, we can do this one of two ways . . . my way, or no way at all!" Of course, I've had to compromise on that attitude every now and then, but I've always found that to be a helpful rule of thumb to live by. The essential point is simply this . . . *you have to seize control.* You have to master your situation. Nothing worth having will ever come your way by accident. You have to make it happen!

Sales Techniques

Many books have been written about the advantages of using various dreamed-up, unproven, and illogical sales techniques. Not only will most of the sales techniques you read about not help you make a sale, they will actually *decrease* your chances of making a sale! I wrote my first book to refute some of the silly, harmful sales techniques I'd heard at a sales seminar.

As I studied the current marketplace in selling skills, I quickly learned that most of the books, tapes, and seminars on sales techniques being sold have no validity whatsoever. While some of the people who advocate these programs might have a sales background, they obviously didn't use the techniques they now teach in the field. They just dreamed them up to sell you books, tapes, and seminars!

Of course, many books, tapes, and seminars were actually dreamed up by people who've never sold anything. The sales techniques I teach were developed and perfected over many years of real selling in the field. They have been refined in the workplace through direct application in countless sales situations. They have produced hundreds of successful salespeople and sales managers. The statistics don't lie. If you work hard and use the sales techniques I teach, you *will* be successful in sales.

When determining whether a technique should be used in a sale, the salesperson should not ask the question, "Can I make it work?" Remember that every tactic works sometimes. Instead, the salesperson's first question should be, "Is this the most effective way to sell my product or service?" Other questions to ask yourself include the following.

1. "Does this technique violate sound principles of salesmanship?" If by chance you don't know what those sound principles are, read my books *Selling* and *Lessons and Adventures in Sales.*

2. "Who came up with the technique or gimmick that I'm considering?" Remember, when you want medical advice, you should only get it from a doctor. If you want advice on cooking, you should get it from a chef. When you want some good advice on salesmanship, you should get it from a professional salesperson. Look closely at that sales book. If it was written by a doctor or a professional motivational speaker, have a good laugh, and then pitch it into the trash bin.

3. "Do I find that I sell better when I use the technique I'm considering, or when I don't use it?" This may seem like a strange question, but you would be amazed at how many salespeople never ask themselves this question when they try out new sales techniques!

4. "Is the technique I'm considering completely honest, or does it involve some degree of deception?" If you decide that any technique would not allow you to be 100 percent honest, then simply don't use it!

5. "When I complete a sale using the technique I'm considering, will I be able to go back and visit this customer as a friend?" This is a simple yes or no question that can be phrased even more simply: Will you be *proud* of the sale? If the answer is no, then don't use the technique!

6. "Does the technique I'm considering require that I manipulate the customer in some way?" Again, if you decide that it does, don't use it. Never try to manipulate

your customers into doing something they would not decide to do on their own.

7. "Will I win? Will my customer win? Will my company win?" Your career in sales won't last for long if you can't answer all three of those questions with an unqualified yes.

8. Managers, listen to your salespeople. A wise man will take good advice even when it comes from a fool. A fool will not take good advice even when it comes from a wise man.

9. No sales technique works every time. Use the sales techniques that your knowledge and experience tell you have the best chance to succeed.

ASKING LEADING QUESTIONS

Many sales techniques include asking your customers leading questions to get them to buy. Some sound clever and effective when they are worded properly. However, basing your sales tactics on asking leading questions is counterproductive, because it simply goes against human nature. Wise men from Confucius to Jesus have told us to treat people the way we want them to treat us. *Nobody* likes to be manipulated by being asked leading questions. This is ultimately a very condescending sales technique that you should avoid in all its various and cleverly packaged forms.

Principles

1. It is *always* counterproductive to ask your customers leading questions. When you force your customer to agree with you on some minor point, you simultaneously force him to guard against buying.

2. Leading questions are a form of manipulation. Don't manipulate your customer . . . educate your customer!

3. Leading questions are insulting. Don't insult your customer . . . edify your customer!

4. Leading questions can evoke resentment, distrust, and evasiveness in customers. Instead, you should work to evoke goodwill, trust, and confidence in customers by talking straight.

5. Only when your customer "knows" your product thoroughly will he be able to make a commitment to it. Make your customer feel as though he *owns* your product or service. Cause him to feel the benefits of owning it. You cannot accomplish this by asking leading questions.

6. Only when you help your customers visualize owning your product or service and reaping all the benefits that it will offer them will they be able to tell you whether or not they can afford what you are offering, how soon they will buy, and how much they will pay.

7. Talk straight with your customers. Let your yes mean yes and your no mean no.

Definitions of Twenty Common Sales Terms

Axiom

An axiom is a statement of a truth that is logical and irrefutable. Axioms are effective tools for salespeople who are making points and refuting a customer's misconceptions. For example, if a customer expresses concerns about the cost of your product or service, a useful axiom might be "Good things are not cheap, and cheap things are not good" (not an Allard original!).

Axioms can be humorous as well as informative. But to be effective, an axiom must be timely, to the point, and delivered convincingly. It's hard for a customer to disagree with a truism that he or she articulates regularly.

As a salesman, I've memorized hundreds of axioms and developed many of my own. Then, I try to always have the best and most appropriate axiom ready to use for any situation I encounter.

Callbacks

Going back to a customer you've already seen once in order to conclude a sale you weren't able to close the first time is called making a callback. If you wish to be a one-call closer, stick to a one-call policy and never make an exception. If you do make exceptions to the "no callback" rule, you will never become strong enough to sell on the first call.

The most important decision I made in my sales career was to *never* make a callback. As most professional salespeople know, it is seductive and tempting to make a callback. You know instinctively that if you put too much pressure on your customer, you'll never make the sale. Your logic tells you that if you give the customer some "space," you can come back later and you might get the sale. You want to make the sale so badly that you lose your resolve and agree to make a callback.

If I could look you in the eye, shake your hand, and give you some advice from my heart, it would be this: Forget your logic. Forget how badly you want or need the sale. Don't even try to figure this out. *Just never make a callback!* (See the chapter "Callbacks and Contingency Sales.")

Close

The close is anything you say or do to get your customer to make a commitment to buy your product or service *now*. The close brings your presentation to its logical conclusion and lets you ask for the order. A good close should result in a sale. The perfect time to close the sale is when your customer knows everything he needs to know to make an intelligent decision and when he is ready to say yes!

The following is one example of a simple and common close: "Mr. Customer, if you will let me put this on order today, I will give you a 10 percent discount. Let's do business!" Closing the sale is payday for commissioned salespeople. You should master the art of closing the sale.

As a salesman in the field, I had three standard closes that I usually used on each customer. If the customer didn't buy after the third close, I would try a fourth that I would base on the customer's particular circumstances. In total, I had eighty-eight closes memorized so I could be prepared for almost any situation I might encounter. I always believed I could sell to anyone if I set my mind to it. However, sometimes it would be like whipping a skunk . . . you can do it, but it's not worth the effort.

Cold Call

When you make a call on a prospect without an appointment to sell your product or service, it is called a cold call. If you can develop a method of selling in this way and can muster the courage to do so, you will have unlimited opportunities to make money. Appointments, by definition, limit your selling opportunities to a certain time and place. When you run out of appointments, you run out of chances to sell.

When you are making cold calls, you can sell your product anytime and anyplace. This form of selling gives you total freedom. There is something magical about spontaneous cold-call selling.

Cold-call selling is the art of salesmanship at its most exciting and creative best. Strong, self-confident salespeople master the art of cold calling and do not like appointments. The truth is, I always resented the term "cold call," because my calls were never "cold"—they were always hot as a firecracker!

Comfort level

Your comfort level is the point in life where all your material needs are met and you feel comfortable and satisfied with the life you and your family are leading. You no longer strive to excel because you think you have all you need. When I first heard about this phenomenon, I did not believe it was real. I could not imagine anyone who didn't want more than what he currently had. Now that I've managed hundreds of salespeople, I not only know it exists, but I've learned to my surprise that, for many salespeople, their "comfort level" is set at a pitifully low level.

Most salespeople work to their needs, not to their opportunities. When I look at the potential that most salespeople have, and then compare it to how little they settle for in life, I am shocked. With just a little more study, practice, hard work, and drive, most $50,000-per-year salespeople could earn at least $100,000. The truth is, most salespeople *never* discover their full potential. Instead, they reach their comfort level and settle into a life of bland mediocrity.

Let me ask you a personal question: Wouldn't you like to find out how good you could be just one time your life? This would be a great time for you to break out of that stale comfort level that has become such a well-worn rut. Exert your energy and creativity, and *excel* as you were meant to do!

Commission

A commission is the money paid to a salesperson for selling a product or service. Commissions are usually based on a percentage of the selling price. The commission percentage paid for selling any product or service is almost always in direct proportion to the difficulty of selling it. Beware of anyone who tells you that his product or service is easy to sell, but it also pays big commissions. The truth is, "there ain't no such animal."

Things that are easy to sell don't pay much. Things that take planning and hard work to sell pay the really big commissions. The secret of making big money in sales is to find something that is truly difficult for others to sell, and then to make yourself the absolute master of selling that product or service. You will then be paid big commissions because you can do something that others find difficult. To salespeople, commissions are like West Virginia: "almost heaven."

Golden handcuffs

Anything that keeps you in a sales position longer than you believe is advisable for you to stay is called a golden handcuff. For example, you might want to leave your position because you are not making enough money, but you don't leave because you don't want to give up your insurance coverage. That insurance is a golden handcuff that keeps you from leaving your position and moving on to something more lucrative.

Company cars, retirement programs, or the promise of a bonus or promotion can all make you reluctant to leave a position and seek a better opportunity elsewhere. Usually, the benefits derived from these things are not worth the price of staying in a bad situation. When you find yourself in a low-paying, boring, dead-end situation that no longer challenges you, don't let golden handcuffs tie you down. Remember, this is your time up at bat! At least take a cut at the ball. Life is an adventure. Live yours to the fullest!

Hype

When you do something to get people excited, usually with the intention of exploiting their excitement to your benefit, it is called hype. Hype is the stock in trade of those who want to take advantage of people. Companies that want to sell you their products or services convince you that you can make big money by selling them to others using hype. They try to convince salespeople that hype is the key that will unlock big money in sales with little effort.

Books, tapes, and seminars promising success, money, and wellbeing also use hype. For some reason, salespeople seem more susceptible to hype than any other group of people. They also seem to be more forgiving of those who take advantage of them, going back time after time for another dose of hype.

Here is a simple and proven technique you can use to protect yourself from hype. When anyone offers you big rewards for little effort or money—when he makes a special offer that seems too good to be true—look at him carefully. If you see that it is neither Santa Claus nor your mama, just say *no!*

Laydown

Salespeople refer to any easy sale as a laydown. If you make enough calls, you are sure to find your share of laydowns. A word of caution about these easy sales is in order here, though. No matter how badly you want or need a sale, you should never take advantage of a weak, uninformed, or gullible customer. It is a true test of your character and your respect for the dignity of your customers when you refuse to exploit another person when no one else is watching.

I do not like or use the term "laydown." I do not think sales managers should encourage its use. I think the term is derogatory and demeaning to the customers whom I respect and upon whom I depend for my income.

Leads

A lead is the name and address of a prospect who, for whatever reason, has been identified as a likely candidate for the product or service you are selling. In my opinion, leads are the most misunderstood and overrated aspect of selling. If you can sell your product or service without leads, you are far ahead of the game. When you sell without leads, you free yourself to sell anytime and anyplace.

Many leads that are generated through telemarketing are not as good as the stranger you would meet on the street. At least the stranger hasn't had a chance to think up reasons to avoid you and not buy. I never liked to work leads, and usually turned them over to less experienced salespeople. In fact, I never looked for easy sales, choosing instead a real challenge to prove that I was as good as I was always telling people I was.

Numbers game

Most sales organizations advocate the idea that selling is a "numbers game." The idea is also taught in most popular sales seminars. Not only is this idea wrong, it is counterproductive.

The core of this idea is that if you make enough sales calls, you are bound to make some sales sooner or later. This idea makes as much sense as saying that if you hit enough golf balls, sooner or later you will become a golf pro. If you consistently hit a golf ball incorrectly, all you are doing is practicing mistakes. In the same way, if you keep making sales calls incorrectly, you're just practicing mistakes.

Telling salespeople that selling is a numbers game, and then sending them out into the field unprepared, is a tactic used by lazy and heartless sales managers. No salesperson has an unlimited supply of time, money, enthusiasm, and confidence, and it is unfair to squander those limited resources with poor training or no training at all. Salespeople should not be required to make sales calls until they are thoroughly prepared for the tasks ahead of them. They should reasonably expect to be able to sell their product or service without having to endure a lot of abuse because they lack the preparation to handle the job.

I've discovered that when I focused more of my energy on training the salespeople I had rather than looking for better salespeople, I was more successful. Remember that a great golf player is the one who can finish the course with the fewest strokes. In the same way, a good salesperson is one who can make successful sales with the fewest calls. If a salesperson does not know how to build value, create urgency and deliver his or her presentation convincingly, they are no closer to a sale after ten calls than they were after the first. If they can do those things, the next call they make will result in a successful sale.

One-call closer

Salespeople who close all of their sales in a single call on their customers are called one-call closers. This may sound like a simple way to do business, but it takes a great deal of planning and courage. There are four essential elements that go into making a one-call sale.

You must *qualify* your customer to make sure you are talking to someone who is empowered to make the buying decision. That decision usually means that the customer has to sign a contract and write you a check without contacting or checking with anyone else. Only a few key people in a business are ever able to make those kinds of decisions on their own.

You must build so much value into your product or service that the customer is willing to do business with you on *your* terms, not his.

You must create urgency. That is, give your customer a compelling and logical reason to buy *now* instead of *later.*

You must have the courage to take a yes or no, never make a callback, and never make any exceptions!

When you combine the cold call and the one-call close,

you have complete freedom to travel, work where and when you want to work, and pay yourself as much as you want to earn. I have sold from Nome, Alaska to New Orleans, from the Golden Gate Bridge to the Brooklyn Bridge, using this method. I have never had a bad day in over twenty years of being a one-call closer.

Overage

The amount of money above the minimum amount for which a product or service could be sold is called overage. Usually, salespeople are paid a higher percentage on the overage than they are paid on the base price of a product or service. Negotiating the purchase price of a product or service is a vital part of every salesperson's job. Most salespeople put too much importance on the price they ask. They drop their price too soon, and by too much. They depend on the price to close the sale for them. The truth is that for a direct salesperson, revealing your price too soon is just like showing your cards prematurely in a poker game.

When my customers would ask me to tell them the price before I was ready to close the sale, I would usually reply with a comment like, "I'm just like you. I'm going to get all I can, so let's start to negotiate." I've found that customers usually respond favorably when you do the right thing, and simply tell them the truth.

Override

An amount of money beyond the sales commission that is paid to salespeople and managers is called an override. The override is usually based on a percentage of their sales together with the sales of all those whom they train and manage. It is important for anyone who qualifies for an override to maintain written documentation that outlines the details of the override remuneration program.

The most common form of fraud perpetrated against salespeople and sales managers is when they are deprived of an agreed-upon override. Such specifics as the amount of override that will be paid, the term of the program, and on whom override compensation will be paid should all be well documented. In addition, any expenses or deductions that will come out of the override should be agreed upon in detail and put down in writing before the override program starts. Another important detail to be settled up front is when the override will be paid.

Unfortunately, too many salespeople have faced the unpleasant realities of building sales for their company assuming they were working under one agreement only to discover that their agreement had been changed without their consent. Be on guard to make sure this never happens to you! Work hard to fulfill all of your agreements and obligations, but always expect the company you represent to do likewise. Finally, remember the old Chinese proverb: "The weakest ink is stronger than the strongest memory." *Write your agreement down!*

Presentation

A sales presentation is the script that the salesperson uses to sell a product or service. A good presentation should contain the following elements.

1. *Complete information.* You must communicate all the information your customers need to make an intelligent decision about buying your product or service.

2. *Value.* Describe the value of your product or service sufficiently to make your customer want to buy. Value is the most important element in the presentation, because value or benefit is the only reason anyone buys anything.

3. *Urgency.* This consists of giving your customer a logical reason to buy *now* instead of *later.*

4. *Clarity.* Usually a customer is given a great deal of information to absorb in a short period of time. The longer I'm in sales, the more important I realize clarity is to successful sales. One thing is certain . . . confused customers almost never buy.

5. *Trust.* You must be believable and trustworthy. The same applies to your product or service, and the company you represent.

6. *Price.* In most sales presentations, the discussion of price is a part of the close. Remember that when the value of your product or service exceeds the price in the mind of your customer, the customer buys.

7. *The close.* This consists of giving your customer a reason to buy now, and then asking for the order. Never forget that the close is payday for direct salespeople, so master the art of closing.

Most new salespeople fail because they don't learn their sales presentations perfectly or practice it until they can deliver it convincingly.

Rejection

The secret to a long career in sales is learning how to deal with rejection. Keep in mind that the customer is not rejecting you, but your offer. The fear of being rejected by customers is a major reason why salespeople fail. Fear of rejection is also the primary reason why people do not go into sales. The good news, and the flip side of this coin, is that rejection is the primary reason why selling pays a lot of money. If everyone wanted to do it, or could do it well, it wouldn't pay very much.

Scam

Any sales tactic that is designed to deceive a customer is a scam. Any sales tactic that does not describe the risks or hidden costs of a product or service is a scam. Any organization that sells a product or service to salespeople for resale, knowing that more people will ultimately lose money than will make money, is also a scam. This includes, in my opinion, *all* multilevel network marketing companies.

The big problem with a scam is that if you run one, you have to live with a crook all of your life. Your spouse is married to a crook. Your children's parent is a crook! And worst of all, you have to brush a crook's teeth, comb a crook's hair, and look at a crook in the mirror every morning.

Spiz man or woman

Salespeople who can be counted on to create excitement by bringing in sales are called spiz men or women. They are usually given the task of motivating new salespeople or instilling new life in a flagging sales team. A spiz salesperson is not necessarily the best salesperson on the team, but a sales manager can depend on him or her the way a baseball coach can depend on a clutch hitter. He or she can be counted on to perform when performance is most needed.

It's difficult to break into direct sales and succeed. There's much to learn, and usually there is little if any income at the start. The most important thing a manager can do for new salespeople is to give them the confidence to believe that if they work hard enough, they can and will succeed. That's where the spiz salesperson comes in. That person shows that it really is possible to bring in the orders, and by bringing in orders, he or she instills much-needed confidence.

The spiz salesperson also benefits. An excellent way to motivate salespeople is to let them show off their orders in front of their peers. (At least I know this tactic always worked on me!)

Urgency

When you give your customer a logical, compelling reason to buy now it is called creating urgency. This can be achieved in many different ways. It can be as subtle as looking at your watch and preparing to leave or as obvious as offering the customer a price discount if he commits to buying now. For example, you might say something like, "Mr. Customer, I cannot come back next week. I am going to be in Pittsburgh. If you will let me put this on order today and save me some time, I will give you $500 off the price." There are many ways to create urgency. Good salespeople should master them all . . . and then think up new ones!

My favorite method for creating urgency is to tell my customers the simple truth about how buying decisions work. I'll say something like, "If you don't buy now, you are going to cool down and you'll never buy. I'm not going to kid myself, and I hope you don't kid yourself. If you don't buy now, you will probably *never* have this product." I will then often add, "And you will *never* get the chance to do business with me again!" For most customers who have already recognized the value of your product or service, the thought of never having it is a much greater inducement to buy than the thought of being able to take their time in making a decision and paying for the product or service later.

Value

Value, sometimes called benefit, is all the good things, either imagined or real, that your customer will personally derive from owning your product or service. The greatest skill you can develop as a salesperson is the ability to build value in the eyes and the mind of your customer. A basic truism of salesmanship is that the only reason anybody ever buys anything is for the value he perceives he will derive from owning it. When the value of a product or service exceeds its price in the mind of the customer, the customer buys. The essence of selling is to discover what is of value to your customer and incorporate that value into your product or service.

There's always a limit on how far you can lower your price, but there is never a limit on how much value you can build. If most salespeople would spend as much time building value as they do trying to close a sale, they would certainly close many more sales.

Family Talk

As you know, I've spent most of my adult life in sales. I first entered this profession in 1959, and began my full-time career as a professional salesman in 1978. (There was a time after my second divorce when I was down on my luck and had to deliver pianos at night . . . but that's another story!) The point is that I have no doubt about what I am or what I was meant to be. I'm a *salesman!* Almost all of my friends are salespeople, and I like to be around them. I consider the salespeople I know to be a part of my family. Well, I'd like to take a moment now to have a little personal talk with all of you whom I think of as family.

I thought it would be appropriate to have this little talk now for three reasons. First, I'm concerned about those New Year's resolutions you made last year. Remember all those splendid resolutions that were going to make this year so special for you? Well, I can't help but wonder whether or not you've done anything to keep them.

Second, I'm a little concerned about your physical, financial, and mental health. I'm worried about you. I want you to be healthy, financially solvent, and mentally strong.

Third, did you hear the news? Your uncle died. You know which uncle I mean. He's the one whose advice you always valued more highly than mine. For years I've been advising you to quit smoking, because if you don't it will inevitably ruin your health. It will shorten your life. While you live, it will diminish the quality of your life. But your uncle, the "Marlboro Man," always used to say, "Sure, I smoke . . . but look at me! Look at what a stud I am!" You listened to him instead of me. Well, he died. I think it was throat cancer from smoking that killed him. I don't want that to happen to you.

All right, let's take a moment to think about the physical, financial, and psychological factors that can have a significant impact on your career and your life.

PHYSICAL

Think back with me now about some of the promises you've made to yourself over the years.

1. You were going to get yourself into the best physical shape of your life.

2. You were going to quit smoking and drinking too much.

3. You promised to lose a lot of weight and lower your cholesterol level.

4. You said to yourself, "I realize that I've only got one body. When it goes, so does everything else." You told yourself that it was time to take action and get yourself into shape, right?

Now, let me ask you a couple of questions that only a close family member would ever have the right to ask. You've made these promises to yourself, but you and I both know you haven't kept them. What's the matter with you? Are you a weakling? Don't you have enough character to do the things you know you should do?

Hey, I know it's tough, but do you really expect me to believe that you don't have the character or the guts to suck it up and take charge of your life? Yeah, I know that you're upset with me right now, cousin, but I can't worry about that. Right now, I'm thinking about how good you are going to feel if I make you angry enough to take action and really get yourself into excellent physical shape!

Within the next few years, many of you who are now reading this will hear words similar to these: "You've got cancer," "You're suffering from emphysema," or "You've had a serious heart attack." Others will hear words along the lines of: "Honey, I'm so glad that you've quit smoking and gotten yourself into such great shape!"

One last point. Do you know what happened when the Marlboro Man died? They just found another rugged-looking actor and dressed him up in a cowboy suit. They gave him a pack of cigarettes, and presto!—they had another Marlboro Man. I'd hate for anybody . . . your boss, your spouse, your children, anybody . . . to ever have to find a replacement for you.

FINANCIAL

Ah yes, money . . . a favorite topic for just about everyone. Remember how you were going to get your finances in order this year?

1. You said that you were going to pay off your debts and you weren't going to buy anything on credit anymore.

2. You said you were going to start a savings plan, and always pay yourself first.

3. You said you were going to stop that stupid gambling.

4. You said that you were going to set aside enough money to pay your taxes, and never let yourself fall behind.

So what happened, my brothers and sisters in sales? Are you on target, or did you get a little sidetracked . . . again?

I'm often appalled by the way I see salespeople handle their money. Salespeople tend to be the freest spenders on earth. I know some salespeople who earn over two hundred thousand dollars a year, and have done so for many years. Despite this, if they were to be out of work for a month of so, they would be totally broke.

I'd like to be a fly on the wall of your home as you sit and work out your financial plans with your spouse. I'll bet your discussion might go something like this. "Honey, we've got a little crisis here," the man tells his wife. "Do you remember how we spent $3,000 last month? Well, we only earned $2,500. Now, this month, we've earned $3,000. If we don't do something drastic soon, we're going to have too much money! What are we going to do?"

"Well, you can count on me," she assures him. "I'll go out tomorrow and spend $2,000, okay?" "Great," the man says, "and I'll spend another $2,000. That'll only put us $1,500 in debt, but every dollar counts. We'll be living like the Joneses soon. We'll be in debt as far as we can possibly go!"

Hey! Get yourself out of debt now! Spend *less* than you earn. Pay yourself first. I know it's not easy, but the quality of your life, for the rest of your life, and the quality of your children's lives depend on your ability to develop the character necessary to "just say no" to unnecessary spending.

Three simple rules that would help assure your financial stability will require a great deal of will power on your part. However, they would also change your life forever. Those rules are:

1. Put 10 percent of your income in the bank and don't touch it. Pay yourself first.

2. *Don't buy anything for which you cannot pay cash* (with the possible exception of a house and car).

3. Buy the things you need, not the things you want, especially if you only want them because someone else has them.

Maybe one day you'll hear your spouse saying, "I just can't take this debt anymore . . . I'm leaving." On the other hand, maybe you could say, "Honey, let's send the kids to Paris for the summer, and you and I can take a little vacation to Las Vegas."

MENTAL

Didn't I hear you say that this was the year in which you were going to really *prepare yourself* for success?

1. You were going to learn and master everything that pertained to your job.

2. You were going to master your sales presentation and learn to deliver it confidently and convincingly.

3. You were going to take courses, read books, and generally do everything you could do to improve yourself and expand your mind.

4. This was supposed to be the year you were going to prepare yourself for a management position.

I don't want to be unkind, but what happened? Did you lose your direction, focus, or resolve? Well, guess what . . . the rewards are still out there if you still have the desire to go after them. You still have the opportunity to make it. Why don't you get yourself back on track right now? You can decide right now what the future will be for you and your loved ones. The choice is entirely your own.

One day your boss might say to you, "Sorry we gave young Tom that position. He's such a hustler. He's learned our business thoroughly, and he really brings in the sales."

Why should other people get the promotion you deserve? Why shouldn't you be the top salesperson or manager in your organization? Why don't you invest the next three months to change your life for the better, a change that will serve you well for the rest of your life? Believe me when I tell you that you'll be glad you did!

The Man with Three Tongues

I am going to tell you a sad but true story. I believe this story contains a valuable lesson for all salespeople.

You have, no doubt, seen a one-legged man and a man with one arm. You have heard about two-faced women and two-headed idiots. You have probably even heard of or seen a three-legged dog. Well, let me tell you about a young man I hired some time ago who was stranger than any of these.

Some time back I hired a young man with three tongues. That's right . . . he had three tongues! Now, having three tongues might seem like a great advantage for a salesperson. After all, talking is our business. The problem was that this young man's different tongues couldn't agree on anything.

One tongue was very positive. It was gung-ho! The other two tongues were always negative. The first tongue said, "I'm going out in my first month and I'm going to make my quota." The other two tongues said, "Let's wait a while and see what happens. We want to find out how everybody else does first."

The first tongue said, "I'm going to make $1,000 this week." The two other tongues said, "No, not this week. There's a holiday this week. Let's wait. We should just go home and study our presentation."

The positive tongue said, "Let's be number one. Let's break records. Let's get promoted." The negative tongues said, "Not now. It won't work. It isn't fair. It's too cold. It's too hot. It's raining. Let's do it later."

This young man talked incessantly about all the things he was going to do to achieve success. However, when it came to doing the work necessary to achieve success, the pair of negative tongues objected. They thought of a million reasons to put off making an effort, or to cut corners, or to simply not do the work at all. This young, talented man failed miserably because his three tongues couldn't agree on anything.

All of us are, at times, like this young man. You see, his positive tongue was in his mouth. His two negative tongues were in his shoes! He "talked the talk," but he didn't "walk the walk." His mouth wrote checks, but his feet weren't willing to cash them. He did too much talking and not enough walking. Have you considered the fact that God gave you one tongue and two feet? Now you know why! You are supposed to do twice as much walking as talking. Well, the time for talking is over. It's time to do some walking.

If I could give new salespeople one piece of advice, it would be this. Rip the tongues out of your shoes the minute they talk back to you. Your feet should be your servants, not your master! Then, every time you think a negative thought, you could look down at your feet and smile. At the same time, take your dictionary and cut out the words *can't* and *quit.* There is nothing you can't do if you don't quit!

I have to be around people who are always coming up with reasons why they can't do things. Then, when they finally motivate themselves to attempt something, they quit before they have a chance to succeed at it. The difference between a winning and a losing effort is *always* the intensity and the duration of the effort. Let's not just talk about success. Let's walk the walk, and work the work. Let's study, prepare, and work until we achieve the success we desire.

THE MAN WITH THREE TONGUES.

Conclusion

When I published my first book, *Selling,* and my second book, *Lessons and Adventures in Sales,* I received some criticism. In those books, I debunked many of the myths that some salespeople had accepted for years as gospel truth. Well, that made some people unhappy with me. I also pointed out some of the scams that are out there taking advantage of salespeople. This made a few con men *very* unhappy! And then, of course, there was this business of calling myself "The King of Salesmen." Well, I can understand the reaction to that. I probably would have felt the same way if someone had beat me to it and done the same thing. I can appreciate how many people felt when they read my books. I don't ask that they all agree with me, only that they consider my ideas with an open mind.

But I haven't only received criticism. I've also received many wonderful letters from salespeople across the country who tell me how my books had changed their lives for the better. These people tell me that when they applied the principles I outlined, they became more successful. They told me that by becoming able to recognize the myths associated with selling and avoiding them, while also applying correct principles, they were now earning much more income than they ever thought possible. For me, however, the most exciting aspect of these letters was the common theme that ran through them all. These salespeople told me that as a result of reading my books, they had developed a tremendous sense of *pride* in their profession, and in themselves.

This is without question the primary reason I write these books. I love selling, and I love salespeople. It is my sincere hope that all salespeople will be helped and inspired by my words, that they will take hold of the many wonderful opportunities that selling presents to make all their dreams come true. I hope you are one of them!